SUMMON MY EHI TO UGBINE

OKPAME ORONSAYE

SUMMON MY EHI TO UGBINE

Bibliografische Information der Deutschen Nationalbibliothek:
Die Deutsche Nationalbibliothek verzeichnet diese Publikation in der
Deutschen Nationalbibliografie; detaillierte bibliografische Daten sind im
Internet über http://dnb.dnb.de abrufbar.

Herstellung und Verlag: BoD – Books on Demand, Norderstedt

ISBN: 978-3-7386-5225-3

PREFACE

PREFACE TO THIRD EDITION

The third edition of Summon My Ehi to Ugbine is primarily due to the acquisition of some information about the events that led to the January 4 1987 incident at Ugbine from the Edo viewpoint,which are coming gradually into light. Iro Eweka in his book, *Dawn to Dusk*, shed some light on the clandestine roles played in the final phase of the events by some high-ranking Edo Ekhaemwen who wanted to 'put the Benin king-Emperor (Omo N'Oba Ovonramwen) in trouble'. He also pointed out the driving force behind the British intentions, which was; "They (the British) had not come to make friends. They came to bully and to rob, to cheat and to steal". Sadly. this truism is what the majority of eminent scholars(American, European and even many African) of African art history and history have refrained from mention in their discourses about the January 4 1987 incident at Ugbine. An incident that they continue claim to be "Benin Massacre".

According to James Russell Lowell, 'Once to every man and nation comes the moment to decide In the strife of Truth with Falsehood, for the good or evil side.' And this moment has arrived for these scholars of African art history and history, including mainstream publications and media to decide whether they are on the side of Truth or Falsehood in their versions of the British intentions, the events that led to the "Benin Massacre", and the destruction and looting of Benin City.

Okpame Osawamienghemwen Oronsaye
January 2020 Wächtersbach, Germany

PREFACE

PREFACE TO SECOND EDITION

After obtaining some fresh information a slight modification has been made on a section of the book Summon My Ehi To Ugbine. Nonetheless, the main text and message remains unchanged. It is, however, worthwhile to mention that even before the publication of Summon My Ehi To Ugbine in 2016, there has been an increasing awareness in America and Europe of the wanton destruction and looting of Benin City in 1897. Indeed much earlier on there have been incessant calls for the return of the Edo people stolen treasures back to the rightful owners. These calls however gathered momentum following the action of one individual, Mr. Mark Walker. In 2014 Mr. Walker, a grandson of one of the soldiers who took part in the gruesome destruction and looting of Benin City, returned two bronzes to the Benin king-emperor, Omo N'Oba Erediauwa (r. 1979-2016). Mr. Walker is reported to have been motivated to return the two bronzes because they were described in his grandfather diary as "loot". Mr. Walker is also reported to have said, " That gave me the idea that perhaps they should go to the place where they will be appreciated for ever."

However, the narratives of the events that lead to the destruction and looting of Benin City as presented by 19th- and 20th century American and European scholars of African art history and history, publications, and mainstream media remains largely unchanged. The fable they created out of the British government official report that several unarmed British official and traders who were on a peaceful trade and mission to the Benin king-emperor were massacred by Benin chiefs continued to be re-echoed. Apparently, this fabrication seems to have become a template on which the narratives of the incident are written. Hence it is not surprising that 130 years after the incident contemporary scholars of African art history and history, publications and mainstream media still present such writings as:

"...British traders were furious that Oba (King) Ovonramwen, ruler of the still independent territory, had defied the empire and was demanding customs duties from them. Outrage back home in the UK was fuelled when a group of officers dispatched to see the Oba on the orders of the governor of Britain west African Niger Coast Protectorate were ambushed and killed." - Museums In Talks To Return Benin Bronzes To Africa. - The Guardian, 12 August 2017.

"In 1897 a British Trading expedition arrived in Nigeria to explore the potential for conducting business with the region for various items such as Palm oil. An initial party of some 9 British officers arrived in Benin City in an attempt to open negotiation with the Oba and his Council of Chiefs. This meeting was a disaster and resulted in the death of the 9 British Naval officers."
- Benin Bronzes. www.richardlander.org.uk

"A London punitive expedition sent to avenge the murder of British envoys conquered Benin City." - Die Magie der Kriegerkönige: Geo Epoche Nr. 66. Afrika 1415- 1960.

PREFACE

Hopefully, in the near future, the actual narratives of the events that lead to the invasion, destruction, and looting of Benin City as mentioned in the book, Summon My Ehi To Ugbine, will be acknowledged by American and European scholars of African art history and history, publications, and mainstream media.

Okpame Osawamienghemwen Oronsaye
August 2017 Wächtersbach, Germany

CONTENT

This book is dedicated to Ologbose Irabor, Ekhaemwen Obakhavbaye, Uso, Obayuwana Obaradesagbon and Oviawe, Okakuo Ebeikhinmwin, Omuada Asoro and all unsung Edo warriors who died fighting the British imperialists between January 1897 and May 1899.
You are not dead. You are honoured Ancestral Spirits

ACKNOWLEDGEMENT

ACKNOWLEDGEMENT

The Edo people of the Midwestern area of Nigeria believe every living thing individual has an ehi (mystical or spirit twin). The *ehi* ensures that the *uhimwen* or self-predestination of an entity lifespan on earth is carried out precisely as the entity had avowed on the day it, he or she was created by *Orisa N'Oghodua*, the supreme creator God. The ehi is thus perceived by the Edo not only as the guide and guard but also a witness to an entity's sojourn on earth.

Ugbine is a small town located a few kilometres west of Benin City on the Benin/Ekewan (Ekiohuan) Road. It was founded in the early 19th century as a farm settlement by Okhaemwen Ogbeide-Oyo, the then *Inneh N' Ibiwe* (a high-ranking functionary in the *Ibiwe* palace guild), hence the name Ugbine (ugbo inneh or Inneh's farm settlement).

Ugbine was thrust into the limelight of European history by an incident that took place there on January 4, 1897, which scholars and experts of African history and art history, mainstream media publications and writers, choose to refer to as the 'Benin Massacre'. The Benin Massacre, in their opinion, was the unprovoked killing of seven unarmed British envoys and traders, who were allegedly on a peaceful mission to Benin City by a group Benin chiefs, whom they claimed were fetish and bloodthirsty savages.

Summon My Ehi To Ugbine, is neither a history reference book nor a critique of any publication of the Ugbine incident. Neither is it a personal nor an Edo view of the events that led to the alleged January 4, 1897 'Benin Massacre' at Ugbine, the subsequent plundering and razing of Benin City and the reign of terror the British unleashed on the Edo people from 1897 to 1899. Summon My Ehi To Ugbine is not an expose of these events. The story has been documented and long told by those who consciously or unconsciously initiated, orchestrated and executed the tragic and painful chapter of Benin history. However for over a century subsequent storytellers: professional historians and art historians, including internationally renowned publications have retold this story, unfortunately sadly shamelessly prejudiced and massively distorted. *Summon My Ehi To Ugbine* is a let-the-truth be heard story. And nothing more.

My sincere gratitude to all, whose material and moral support brought this work to fruition especially, my mother Princess (Dr) Aiyevbekpen Katherine Oronsaye, my brothers and sister, Professor Jude Oronsaye, Mr. Patrick

ACKNOWLEDGEMENT

Oronsaye, Mr. Leonard Oronsaye, Ms. Consolata Oronsaye, and Mr. Damian Oronsaye, my cousins Prince Bruce Ailobafe Eweka and Prince Osahon Ogbonmwan Eweka, and my friends Dr. Sam Osarenkhoe and Mrs. Charlotte Osarenkhoe.

My heartfelt thanks to Mr Richard Ayanru who took, time to proofread the final manuscript.

My sincere thanks to Edo commentators, writers, and musicians, whose views of the Ugbine incident was food for thought. My deepest gratitude to the honest non-Edo critics, writers, and historians, who cherish and hold truth sacred, whose unbiased and objective reports helped in the search for the true account of the events that led to the Ugbine incident, and the plundering and razing of Benin City.

Okpame Osawamienghemwen Oronsaye
January 2016 Wächtersbach, Germany

'*If you tell a lie big enough and keep repeating it people will eventually come to believe it.*'

- Joseph Goebbel, Nazi Propaganda Minister. (1933-1945)

HIS STORY: UGBINE, JANUARY 4, 1897

1897 Jan. 16: Capt. H.L. Gallwey, Vice Consul to Foreign Office. Reporting disaster to and failure of the Benin Expedition. CSO 3/4/1 Vol. 7. p. 1.
1897 Jan. 21: Capt. H.L. Gallwey to Foreign Office. Reporting the disaster to pacific Expedition to Benin. CSO 3/4/1 Vol. 7, p. 18.

On January 10, 1897, an urgent telegram was dispatched from the British Colony of Lagos to the British Foreign Office in London. According to the message, on January 4, 1897, the acting Commissioner and Consul-General of the Niger Coast Protectorate, Mr James Robert Phillips, and several British officials and traders on a diplomatic mission to Benin City, the capital of Benin Kingdom, were ambushed by a group of Benin chiefs. The message went on further to state that the British men, including their African porters, were taken to the city and sacrificed to the gods of the Benin king. In response to this incident, which became universally known as the 'Benin Massacre', the British government declared war on the kingdom of Benin. On 19 February 1897, a combined British Navy and Niger Coast Protectorate Force code-named 'Benin Punitive Expedition' captured Benin City. The city was plundered, and two days later the palace and royal quarters were burnt down.

Essentially for more than a century, writers, historians, especially those acclaimed as 'eminent scholars and experts' of African art history and history, and mainstream publications have upheld the British government official position that Mr Phillips was on a peaceful and unarmed official mission to the king of Benin, which was, 'Phillips as acting Consul-General had to pay a necessary visit to the Benin King in order to avoid resorting to the use of force and complete every peaceful means towards resolving the economic and political impasse in the Benin River region'.

While some of these historians, publications, and writers argued Phillips mission was a diplomatic undertaking, which was made up solely of British envoys, others contended that the mission was a trade venture, which was made up solely of British traders. Some writers and publications even went on further to claim that the mission was a humanitarian venture. In the book *Great Benin: Its Customs Art and Horrors*, it is claimed, 'Phillips was determined on a peaceful mission' and the *International Herald Tribune* in its January 13,

1897, issue stated, 'The (Phillips) expedition was quite unarmed and was endeavouring to enter by peaceful means the king's city (Benin)'. In some books and publications such as *Treasures of Ancient Nigeria, Black Africa: Masks, Sculpture and Jewellery*, and *Encyclopaedia Britannica* (1911 edition) the assertions are that Phillips was on a routine visit to the king of Benin. And some other publications such as, *Royal Art of Benin: The Perls Collections* and *The Story of Nigeria*, the contention is that Phillips was on a mission to discuss trade agreement with the Benin king, and while in the book, *Benin: Kings and Rituals* the contention is, '... it (Phillips party) was a peaceful mission, which wanted to persuade King Ovonramwen to keep to the terms of trade agreement that was concluded in 1892'. While in its January 16.1897 publication, *The New York Times* claimed that the Phillips party was a 'British Commercial Expedition'.

The *Time Magazine* in an article, 'City of Blood', in its December 16, 1935, issue, portrayed these views colourfully. And according to the publication, 'Britain was eager to trade with forbidden Benin in the interior and acting Consul General Phillips had sent a message to grinning black King Overami (Ovonramwen) of Benin, asking permission to visit his capital to arrange a treaty'.

Some publications, however, contend that Phillips was on a mission to demand an end to the customs duties collected from British traders by the Benin king. And as stated by *The New York Times* in its January 22, 1897 issue, 'the Phillips mission was to persuade the Benin king, who had threatened death to any white men who attempted to visit him, to remove obstacles he was putting the way of trade'.

However, in an article, *Benin: The Sack That Never Was*, the writer claimed, 'A large part of the purpose of the Expedition (Phillips) was to suppress the practice of human sacrifice'. And this was the same view adopted by the *Time Magazine*, in the article 'The Bronzes of Benin' in its August 6 1965 issue, which was, 'Objecting to the sale of slaves and human sacrifice, a consul general set out in 1897 with eight men to halt the annual ritual of slaughter'. This alleged humanitarian mission was further amplified in the book, *The Village of Ghosts* where it is claimed, 'Phillips was appalled by the human sacrifice in Benin City and was determined to visit Benin City and persuade the Benin king to abolish it'. Even, according to a Nigerian researcher, U.O.A. Esse, 'The conquest of Benin in 1897 completed the British occupation of south-western Nigeria. The incident that sparked the expedition (Benin Punitive Expedition) was the massacre of a British consul and his party, which was on its way to investigate reports of ritual human sacrifice in the city of Benin'. Then one other publication claimed, 'In 1896 a small armed force from the Oil River Protectorate led by the governor entered Bini (Benin) territory to talk to their ruler about ending slavery and human sacrifice...' Incidentally Captain Boisragon, Commandant of the Niger Coast Protectorate Force and one of the survivors of the alleged 'Benin Massacre', in his book, *The Benin Massacre*, wrote: 'The object to the expedition was to try and persuade the king to let the white men come up to his city whenever they wanted to'.

Many writers, historians, and publications also alleged that Phillips sent messages to the Benin king asking for permission to visit Benin City. While some accounts contend that Phillips sent his message to the Benin king from Sapele, some others maintained that Phillips' message was sent from Ughoton (Gwato) in early January 1897 when he was already on his way to Benin City. There are accounts, which also argued that Phillips and the Benin king even exchanged a couple of messages. And as to the alleged response of the Benin king to Phillips' purported message or messages, again there are diverging opinions. While some publications claim that the Benin king after receiving the message asked Phillips to postpone his visit, some contend the Benin king rejected Phillips' request. According to one publication, it is claimed, 'Messengers had been sent to the king, conveying presents, and acquainting him of the Consul-General's proposed visit; the reply brought back was friendly, but the king requested that the white men postpone their visit for two months until the annual ceremony, or what he called 'making his father' (i.e. performing sacrifices at his father's grave), was over. The Consul-General then sent to say that he could not wait, but would come at once. The king replied that he would receive the Mission.' In another publication, the contention was: '... initially, the Benin king said that he could not receive the officials as he was making "Juju" but later he agreed to meet them at Benin after the importance of the mission was explained to him'. There are also claims that Phillips embarked on his ill-fated mission without waiting for the Benin king's reply.

The assertion by historians, writers, and publications that the British envoys and traders were deliberately massacred by Benin chiefs allegedly sent by the Benin king to receive and escort them into Benin City also has different versions. While some historians and writers alleged that the British envoys and traders were killed because at that time of year the Benin king was performing some rituals and hence could not be seen by foreigners, there are those who insist that the envoys and traders were murdered because the Benin chiefs did not want them to witness the mass execution of slaves. This version was again dramatised by the *Time Magazine* in the article, 'City of Blood', where it is stated, '… grinning King Overami did not want Consul Phillips to enter his town because for three months he and his chieftains had been slaughtering living slaves in memory of the dead King Adolor'. And according to the author of *The Village of Ghosts*, '… the group of chiefs who were sent to conduct them (Phillips' Party) into Benin City had no intention of doing so. They were bitterly angry that these Europeans should come so arrogantly into their country in this way and had decided to kill them. Ominously, the chief responsible for sacrificial victims accompanied the (Benin) war party'.

The impression that the Benin people are bloodthirsty savages was further intensified by some writers, art historians and historians, and publications. For instance, *The New York Times* in its 22 January 1897 issue claimed, 'the members (of the British Expedition) went unarmed into a Savage Country, and were ambushed and killed without mercy'. While in the article, *The Oba's Palace: Historical Accounts*, the writer claims, 'In 1897 a party of British traders entered the lands of Benin only to be ambushed and massacred'. And in the book *Benin: Kings and Rituals*, the contention is, '… members of the Phillips mission… were killed against all rules of hospitality and conventions of international relationship'.

There are however some publications and writers who argued that the British envoys and traders were killed because they tried to force their way into Benin City. One writer contends that members of the Phillips mission were killed because the Benin chiefs thought the European party coming to Benin City to wage war on the Oba. There are also two popular Benin people versions of the incidence. One version claims the British envoys and traders were killed because they were bringing a white bride for the Benin king, while the other version has it that the white men were killed because the 'big' (high-ranking) chiefs wanted to 'put the Benin king in trouble'.

Although in recent years some articles and publications have contended that the Benin Punitive Expedition was undertaken for British political and economic interests, there remain huge gaps in their accounts. The truth about the events leading to Phillips mission, his intentions, his group's composition are still being suppressed, and even more, the carnage, especially the deliberate burning of the royal palace, which took place in Benin City between the 19 and 21 February 1897 continued to be denied.

THE EUROPEANS: FRIENDS & FOES

THE EUROPEANS: FRIENDS & FOES

'*... I am a friend of the Benin king.*'-*Durate Pacheco Pereira, Portuguese Chronicler. 1504.*
'*... The great stumbling block to any immediate advance being the fetish reign of terror which exist throughout the kingdom of Benin and will require severe measures in the future...*' - *Major (later Sir) Claude Maxwell MacDonald, British Consul, Oil River Protectorate. 1893.*

They were hardy and daring seafarers, who in equally tough vessels known as Caravels, driven by a combination of religious zeal, trade, and lust for adventure, set out of the south-western corner of Europe and opened a new chapter in European history. Although European historians would honour the legendary ones such as Bartholomew Diaz, the first European to reach the Cape of Good Hope the southern tip of Africa (1488), Vasco Da Gama, who commanded an expedition to find the sea route to India around the Cape of Good Hope (1497) and Pedro Alvarez Cabral who made Brazil a Portuguese possession (1500), there were men before them, although lesser-known but equally brave and if not more daring. They were the men who took the tentative steps beyond the Canaries Islands and made contact with Black African kingdoms on the West African coastline. About 1472, one of these daring Portuguese, Ruy de Sequeira saileOmo N'Obad up an inlet (which the Portuguese named Rio Formosa, the Beautiful River, but later became known as the Benin River) over three thousand kilometres east of the Cape Verde Islands. Ruy de Sequeira became the first European to reach a West African kingdom that became, known as Beny (Benin). In 1486, another Portuguese seafarer, Joao Alfonso de Aveiro, probably set foot in the kingdom's capital city, Benin City, and the encounter opened Africa's greatest rain forest kingdom to subsequent interactions with Europeans. Although the Portuguese main objective was to trade with the Orient, they were able to establish their presence in a number of areas in the West and Central African coastline, either by guile or brute force, where they began the rape of Africa.

In Benin, the Portuguese who became known as *Ebo Ikpotoki* by the Edo people, won a considerable number of Christian converts including members of the ruling class, built churches and even provided mercenaries for some of the kingdom's military campaigns. Although the Portuguese efforts to assimilate Benin kingdom did not yield the desired result, the Benin/Portuguese relationship was to have some long-lasting impact on many aspects of Benin's political, religious and social structure. Benin adopted the Portuguese language as the language of commerce in transactions with other Europeans. Indeed several Edo words such as *ekuye* (spoon), *ekalaka* (drinking glass) and *alimoi* (orange) are derived from the Portuguese words *colher*, *caneca* and *limo* respectively. Some Benin palace guilds, such as *Iwebo*, *Iwoki* and *Ewua*, and even palace titles such as *Aragua* and *Ohuoba* were all created as a result of this relationship, and to the extent, a residential area, *idunmwun ebo* (European quarter), was created for the Portuguese missionaries and traders in Benin City. The Portuguese monopoly in Benin was broken by the arrival of English seafarers, notably Captain Windam, John Bird, John Newton and James Welsh. And from 1553 to 1590 there was a substantial pepper trade between the Benin Kingdom and the English seafarers. But the relationship ended abruptly because during this period Benin was not actively engaged in slave trafficking, and since the English traders did not find the Pepper Expeditions as profitable as slave trafficking they shifted their attention to the more profitable slave marts on the West African coastline.

In the 17th century, the Dutch embarked on the seizure of all trading ports, especially slaving marts, on the West African coastline. It was a remarkable feat, which however they could not achieve in the Benin trading ports of Gwato (*Ughoton*) and Lagos (*Eko*). The Dutch, like their Portuguese and English predecessors, recognised that Benin trading policies could not be influenced easily but were able to grasp the extent of the kingdom's resources and economic potential. Unlike the English who shifted their attention elsewhere, the Dutch opted to stay, and they remained Benin's major trading partner for over a century. Since they were solely concerned about their commercial pursuits, the Dutch left no enduring influence in Benin but it was their accounts about the kingdom's economic prospects that without doubt kindled the interest of other European nations in Benin kingdom.

In the early 1700, the British and the French wrestled control of West African slave marts from the Dutch, and broke the Dutch monopoly in Benin. In 1788, Captain Jean-Francois Landolphe, a French explorer, after several visits to Benin City was able to establish a factory or trading post for the French Compagnie d'Oywhere on the island of Borodo, on the left bank of the mouth of the Benin River, close to the Benin port of Gwato. In 1792 the French trading post was bombarded and destroyed by the British Navy. The British contention was: 'to prevent the progress of a new colony'. The rivalry between the British and the French helped to a very great extent in disrupting trade in the region and prevented Benin kingdom from establishing permanent trade ties with other seafaring nations.

In the mid 19th century, the British Navy increased the frequency of her incursions along the West African Atlantic coastline, and under the pretext of suppressing slave trafficking, the British began carving out colonies along the coastline. In the 1840s, John Beecroft, the British Consul for the Bights of Benin and Biafra, pushed for the British government takeover of the city-states and kingdoms in the Lower Guinea. In 1850 he intervened directly in the internal affairs of the Benin colony of Lagos (Eko), citing that Kosoko, the *Eleko* (King) of Lagos, as the biggest obstacle in suppressing the slave trade. The intervention led to a civil war in Lagos, and by the mid-1860s Lagos was effectively a British colony. And from their base in Lagos, the British Colonial Authority, with the help of European traders and Christian missionaries, began meddling in the affairs of the *Egba, Ijebu, Ijesha* and *Ilesha* peoples, and ultimately led to another civil war in the region. Except for Ijebu Ode, which the British attacked and captured in 1892 for 'refusing to allow in Christian missionaries', the civil war made it easy for the British to annex many of the Yoruba-speaking city-states without firing a shot.

In Beecroft's tradition, successive British Consuls pursued the annexation of city-states and kingdoms in the Niger Delta region with vigour. Under the guise of offering friendship, British officials effectively deprived the unsuspecting indigenous rulers of their sovereignty by coaxing them into signing custom-made documents, which they called 'Treaties'. In fact, many city-states and communities lost their autonomy even without their rulers signing any 'Treaty'. They were simply unfortunate to be within or in the vicinity of the area the British claimed as their 'Protectorate'. As a rule, any ruler who refused to sign a Treaty or refused the entry of European traders and missionaries into his domain was accused by the Protectorate officials of either obstructing trade or engaged in slave trafficking. Sooner or later the British Navy, the Niger Coast Protectorate's Force or Royal Niger Company Constabulary would embark on a 'Punitive Expedition' to loot and burn down the ruler's town or city-state, and hang him or (if fortunate) sent into exile. Indeed between 1894 and December 1896, the Niger Coast Protectorate carried out scores of such murderous and barbaric pillaging campaigns that they referred to as 'Punitive Expeditions' in the Benin River region including the *Urhobo, Isoko* and *Kwale* heartlands. Several of the looted artefacts, religious and sacred objects of these unfortunate towns and communities are presently on display in many British museums.

Benin kingdom became a subject of intense British interest following a request by Omo N'Oba (king-emperor) Adolor (r. c. 1848-1888) to the British Colonial authorities in Lagos through Captain Richard Burton, an English adventurer who visited Benin City in 1862. Omo N'Oba Adolor had asked the British Colonial authorities to establish a trading post at Gwato. However several visits between 1869 and 1888 by various British officials and traders such as Vice-Consuls Annesley and Blair, Mr Cyril Punch, Mr Bey and the agents of Miller Brothers Company, yielded no positive results. This being so because the British officials and traders were not actually interested in establishing any trading post in Gwato. The officials primary objective was obtaining a 'Treaty' that would make Benin kingdom a protectorate, while the traders were searching for opportunities to dictate and control trade in Benin kingdom.

Fortunately for the British imperialist and traders during this period, there was no reigning *Olu* (king) in *Itsekiri* kingdom, Benin kingdom's immediate south-western neighbour. In the mid-1840s *Olu* Akengbuwa, the *Itsekiri* king, expelled his *Uwangue* (The kingdom's official who was in charge of trade with the Europeans) from his domain The Uwangue sought refuge within Benin territories at Ugbine but the *Olu* continued to harass him. Eventually, the Uwangue appealed to Omo N'Oba Osemwende (r. c. 1816-1848) for protection. The Omo N'Oba sent a message to *Olu* Akengbuwa to desist from troubling the *Uwangue* but the *Olu* replied the Omo N'Oba in a rather unbecoming manner. The Omo N'Oba cursed him and his descendants, and when Olu Akengbuwa died in the late 1840 none of his heirs survived long on the throne. They died in quick succession. Consequently, no *Olu* was enthroned in *Itsekiri* kingdom until the coronation of Iginua II in 1936.

Since there was no *Olu* and hence a central authority in *Itsekiri* territories, the prominent *Itsekiri* nobles and princes began creating fiefdoms for themselves. Some of them, with the appropriate gifts and tributes, obtained permission from the Omo N'Oba of Benin to establish trading settlements in the Benin River area. *Siluko* on the Siluko River and *Sokponba* (Sapoba) on the *Igbaghon* River (Jamieson River) were two of such trading communities in Benin territories. Chiefs Akpasigha and Dudu established *Sokponba* and *Siluko*, respectively, with Omo N'Oba Ovonramwen's permission. The chaotic state of affairs in *Itsekiri* kingdom provided an ideal environment for the British officials and traders to establish and consolidate their presence. Thus it was relatively easy for British officials to establish political control and implement their divide and rule policy by creating puppet rulers whom, they called 'Chiefs'. The British traders too were able to conduct trade on their terms with individual *Itsekiri* traders, and consequently were not subjected to any kind of local duties or levies. Furthermore, they financed and encouraged their *Itsekiri* trading partners to fix prices primarily to disrupt the traditional trading practices in the entire region.

In June 1885 Britain declared a 'Protectorate of Niger District' on all territories between the British Colony of Lagos and the Niger River, however, British officials attempt to sign a 'treaty' with Benin kingdom was interrupted by the death of Omo N'Oba Adolor in 1888. At the end of the lengthy Benin royal funeral and coronation ceremonies in 1891 the newly enthroned Omo N'Oba, who assumed the title *Ovonramwen no gbae isi* (The radiance of the morning sun that covers the realms), was not keen on any relationship with the British officials because it was obvious they had no intention of establishing a trading post in Gwato. Since their real motives were not defined, the Benin king was quite apprehensive of their presence in the region especially following Thompson Oyibodudu, (the sacrificial victim during the 1891 *ugie ivie*, royal coral beads rituals, reaffirmation of Omo N'Oba Ewuare I (r. c. 1440-1473) ominous prediction that one day the white man would come to Benin City and take away a Benin king.

The Omo N'Oba's immediate preoccupation, however, was the renovation of some sections of the palace, which had been in ruins for over seventy years. In 1815 prince Ogbebor usurped the Benin throne following the passing away of Omo N'Oba Obanosa (r. c. 1804-1815). In 1816 Ogbebor lost the 1815/1816 civil hostilities to his half-brother Prince Erediauwa, he set the palace on fire, and then committed suicide. The fire destroyed large sections of the palace, and the victorious Erediauwa, who took the title Osemwende, apparently had no time to restore the palace to its former splendour. Odin-Ovba, his son and successor, who took the title Adolor, was also unable to do so because he spent most of his time suppressing the unrest started by Ogbewekon, his half-brother, and subduing rebellious vassal towns and city-states mostly in the kingdom's western provinces.

In any case, some of the vital materials, such as copper Manilla and iron-roofing sheets, which Omo N'Oba Ovonramwen needed for the project were available only from the *Itsekiri* trading chiefs, because at the point in time Benin was not engaged in any commerce with the European trading firms in the Benin River area. But as soon as the project began, Nana Olumo, the most influential *Itsekiri* trader in the Benin River region, for no apparent reasons, imposed a trade embargo on Benin kingdom. Nana Olumo's rise to prominence in *Itsekiri* territories was largely due to Mr H. Johnston, the British Consul of the Oil Rivers Protectorate that was created in 1890. In 1885 the Consul appointed Nana, 'governor' of the Benin River, in line with the British divide and rule policy, which was explicitly aimed at stirring up hostilities between the *Itsekiri* people and their neighbours. So as the darling of the Protectorate Authority and European traders on the Benin River District, Nana, now addressed as 'Chief', was able to create a trade monopoly with the hinterland. Chief Nana's embargo severely hampered the reconstruction of the king's palace, and also the kingdom's daily routine since she was totally dependent on the *Itsekiri* trading chiefs for the supply of sea salt. Omo N'Oba Ovonramwen did not react rashly to Nana's trade embargo but resolved to end Benin's dependency on Nana or other *Itsekiri* trading chiefs. Consequently, contact was made directly with the European trading firms operating in the region for the procurement of the building material and sea salt, and in due course, modest transactions began with Miller Brothers Company and an independent trader, Mr Cyril Punch.

Cyril Punch was actually a British agent who first visited Benin City in the company of Vice-Consul Annesley during the obsequies of Omo N'Oba Adolor in 1888. During his frequent trading or rather intelligence gathering, 'visits' to Benin City Mr Punch became close to Egiebor, the *Uwangue*, leader of the *Iwebo* palace society and Omo N'Oba Ovonramwen's closest confidant. Without doubt Punch's 'friendship' with the *Uwangue* played a substantial part in convincing Omo N'Oba Ovonramwen, despite his reservations about the white man, to receive an Oil Rivers (later Niger Coast) Protectorate official. Omo N'Oba Ovonramwen believed the British official was coming to discuss trade with a view of opening a trading post within Benin territories. In March 1892 Captain Henry Gallwey, the Vice-Consul of Benin River District, came to Benin City ostensibly to discuss a trade agreement. The Vice-Consul's real motive, however, was quite different. His primary objective was to make Benin kingdom a British Protectorate and get the Benin King to open up his Kingdom to British traders. Hence Gallwey had a ready-made document or 'Treaty'. And the document read:

Article I. Her Majesty the Queen of Great Britain and Ireland, Empress of India, in compliance with the request of the King of Benin, hereby undertakes to extend to him, and to the territory under his authority and jurisdiction, her gracious favour and protection.

Article II. The King of Benin agrees and promises to refrain from entering into any correspondence, Agreement, or Treaty with any foreign nation or Power, except with the knowledge and sanction of Her Britannic Majesty's Government.

Article III. It is agreed that full and exclusive jurisdiction, civil and criminal, over British subjects and their property in the territory of Benin, is reserved to Her Britannic Majesty, to be exercised by such consular or other officers, as Her Majesty shall appoint for that purpose. The same jurisdiction is likewise reserved to Her Majesty in the said territory of Benin over foreign subjects enjoying British protection, who shall be deemed to be included in the expression " British subject" throughout this Treaty.

Article IV. All disputes between the King of Benin and other Kings and Chiefs or between him and British or foreign traders, or between the aforesaid King and neighbouring tribes, which cannot be settled amicably between the two parties, shall be submitted to the British consular or other officers appointed by Her Britannic Majesty to exercise jurisdiction in the Benin territories for arbitration and decision, or for arrangement.

Article V. The King of Benin hereby engages to assist the British consular or other officers in the execution of such duties as may be assigned to them; and, further, to act upon their advice in matters relating to the administration of justice, the development of the resources of the country, the interest of commerce, or in any other matter in relation to peace, order, and good government, and the general progress of civilization.

Article VI. The subjects and citizens of all countries may freely carry on trade in every part of the territories of the King, party hereto, and may have houses and factories therein.

Article VII. All ministers of the Christian religion shall be permitted to reside and exercise their calling within the territories of the aforesaid King, who hereby guarantees to them full protection. All forms of religious worship and religious ordinances may be exercised within the territories of the aforesaid King, and no hindrance shall be offered thereto.

Article VIII. If any vessels should be wrecked within the Benin territories, the King will give them all the assistance in his power, will secure them from plunder, and also recover and deliver to the owners or agents all the property which can be saved. If there are no such owners or agents on the spot, then the said property shall be delivered to the British consular or other officer. The King further engages to do all in his power to protect the persons and property of the officers, crew, and others on board such wrecked vessel. All claims for salvage dues in such cases shall, if disputed, be referred to the British consular or other officer for arbitration and decision.

When the document was translated to Omo N'Oba Ovonramwen, he refused to endorse it. The treaty actually confirmed the suspicions that the British had a hidden agenda because no references whatsoever were made to trade or the establishment of a trading post within Benin territories. In response to the British deceitful ploy, Omo N'Oba Ovonramwen issued an edict barring all white men from entering Benin territories.

The Omo N'Oba's rejection of the Gallwey's document was a major setback for the Protectorate officials and the European traders because it denied them the vital foothold they needed to penetrate the hinterland. Nonetheless Major (later Sir) Claude Maxwell MacDonald, the Protectorate's Consul-General, deemed the Gallwey's document a legal and binding accord because, in his view, Benin kingdom was within the so-called 'British Protectorate of Niger District', which the British imperialist had created in 1885. Consequently, he considered the Omo N'Oba's refusal to endorse the treaty a hostile act and began contemplating how to get rid of the Benin king. According to the *London Gazette* issue of 16 May 1893, Major MacDonald is quoted as saying, '...The great stumbling block to any immediate advance being the fetish reign of terror which exist throughout the kingdom of Benin and will require severe measures in the future before it can be stopped'.

Then in 1894, the already disquieting mood in the Benin River region was worsened when Chief Nana Olumo's erstwhile 'friends', i.e. the Protectorate authority and European traders decided he had outlived his usefulness because he had become too powerful and independent. Consequently, the Protectorate authority accused Nana of operating a trade monopoly, slave trafficking (a business which their new darlings Chiefs Dogho and Dudu were actively practising) and hampering trade in the Benin River District. After some sabre-rattling, in October 1894, a combined British Royal Navy and Niger Coast Protectorate Force under Rear Admiral Frederick Bedford, and Major Ralph Moor, the new Consul-General of the Protectorate invaded Brohiemie, (Ebrohimi) Nana's trading settlement. The settlement was looted and razed. Nana escaped but later surrendered to the British authority in the Colony of Lagos, who then handed him over to the Niger Coast Protectorate. Major Ralph Moor promptly exiled him to the Gold Coast (present-day Ghana)

The senseless and wanton looting and destruction of Brohiemie, and Nana's banishment only served to increase Benin kingdom's apprehension and mistrust for all Europeans. Then, worse still, later in the year, Mr McTaggart, an agent of the Royal Niger Company, unannounced and uninvited, entered Benin City with an armed escort on a 'friendly' visit hoping to persuade Omo N'Oba Ovonramwen to sign a Treaty with the Company. The Niger Coast Protectorate was not pleased with Mr McTaggart's mission, and the Consul-General Sir Ralph Moor lodged a formal protest with the Royal Niger Company. The October 21, 1894, Niger Coast Protectorate official dispatch CSO. 3/1/3, pp. 86-89 reports, Sir Ralph Moor to Foreign Office. Forwarding more reports on the Royal Niger Company's Expeditionary Force into the Protectorate, confirms this formal protest.

In Benin, Mr McTaggart's unannounced, uninvited and armed visit was the final act that convinced Omo N'Oba Ovonramwen the white men were not to be trusted. Consequently, he ordered the closure of all roads leading from the coast to Benin City as a precaution against any sneak armed attack by the white men. Accordingly military encampments were established at Ugbine, Gele-Gele (Gilli-Gilli) near Ughoton and Ologbo, and so after about four hundred years of peaceful trade and social interaction with Europeans, the kingdom of Benin closed her doors to the white man because of the deceit, greed, and intrigues of the British that became, known to the Edo people as *Ebo Oyikpata*, the thieving white man.

Indeed, immediately, after the invasion and destruction of Brohiemie, Consul General MacDonald had contemplated invading the Benin Kingdom in early 1895. Apparently, the British Foreign had advised that pacific means should be employed in the Niger Coast Protectorate self-created dispute with Benin kingdom. Notwithstanding, the new Consul-General, Major Ralph Moor, embarked on clandestine missions to forcibly 'open the roads' to Benin City. He was convinced in his self-righteousness that, '... the Benin king fetish influence was the single major obstacle in the Niger Coast Protectorate's path in the entire region'. In early September 1895, Major Peter Copland-Crawford, the Vice-Consul of Benin District, made the first attempt to 'open the roads' i.e. invade and bring Benin kingdom under British rule. His clandestine invasion force ran into a Benin border guards outpost on the outskirts of Gele-Gele. Confronted by battle-ready Benin border guards, some who were armed with Snider rifles, the Vice-Consul wisely withdrew his invasion force. The September 12, 1895, Niger Coast Protectorate official dispatch CSO 3/2/1, pp. 145-148 reports; Sir Ralph Moor to Foreign Office. Reporting on the abortive Expedition into Benin is a testimony to the attempt. This incident prompted the Protectorate authority's surprise search for rifles and ammunition, in the premises of Messrs Bey and Zimmer trading company in October 1895. The German-owned company was suspected of carrying out clandestine arms trade with Benin kingdom. The October 19, 1895, Niger Coast Protectorate official dispatch CSO 3/2/1, p. 152 reports; Sir Ralph Moor to Foreign Office. Reporting a surprise search of Messrs Bey and Zimmer's premises in Benin for rifles and ammunition confirms this incident.

Then again in December 1895 and June/July 1896, the Niger Coast Protectorate officials made two clandestine abortive attempts to "open the roads". The first was led by Mr Ralph Locke, the vice-Consul of Benin district, and the second by Captain Arthur I. Maling, Commandant of the Niger Coast Protectorate Force detachment based in Sapele. On each occasion, the intruders were met by armed Benin border guards and were forced to withdraw back to their base in Sapele.

During this period Omo N'Oba Ovonramwen was much preoccupied with resolving some of his kingdom's domestic problems. In 1895 when the *Onojie* (Viceroy) of Ekpoma, a town about 50 kilometres North-east of Benin City, died, the elders and people made an unusual request to the Omo N'Oba, saying they no longer wanted an *Onojie* to rule over them. The situation was eventually resolved by coercion when all diplomatic effort to solve the crisis failed: the Omo N'Oba dispatched five special envoys to Ekpoma to enforce the installation of the *Onojie's* heir apparent as ruler. Then later in the year, *Uwangue* Egiebor was murdered, and an enquiry revealed that the murder was planned and carried out by some high-ranking members of the *Iwebo* palace society. In view of her domestic problems and the attempted armed incursions by the British, there was an increased and tighter control of the kingdom's southern borders. Consequently, there was a substantial disruption of the oil palm trade between Benin and *Itsekiri* trading chiefs.

PETITIONS: MARAUDERS & MERCHANTS

'... the petty king of Benin and his Juju men, need to be transported somewhere else...'
-James Pinnock (British trader), June 1896.
' ... there is an immediate prospect of large returns from trade within Benin territory immediately the Protectorate take steps to 'open up' Benin territory' - The principal agent of African Association Limited, October 1896.

Towards the end of 1895 *Itsekiri* traders, under pressure from their European financiers, resorted to price-fixing in their transactions with Benin oil palm produce suppliers. Usually, Benin's trading practice restricted foreign traders to certain trading centres where an *ukoba*, a Benin palace functionary, grant them rights of entry and trade. The *ukoba* also fixed market prices, customs duties and tributes at his discretion, and the traders were only allowed to begin transactions after they had paid all necessary dues. In March 1896, Omo N'Oba Ovonramwen ordered a restriction of oil palm produce supplies to *Itsekiri* traders when reports reached him that they were fixing prices, and also were no longer willing to pay the obligatory dues and tributes. The Omo N'Oba's edict alarmed the European traders because the oil palm trading season, which usually lasted for about four months, was just beginning, and so they urged their *Itsekiri* trading partners to send the 'appropriate gifts and tributes' to the Omo N'Oba to persuade him to lift the restriction and also allow establishment of more trading settlements. Accordingly the *Itsekiri* traders sent a messenger with gifts worth about forty-pounds sterling (£40) to Benin but apparently the gifts did not impress the district's *ukoba*, bearing in mind that a puncheon (about 70 gallons or 318 litres) of oil palm produce was worth about eight pounds sterling (£8), and so he refused the messenger entry into Benin territory. The Omo N'Oba, on learning of the *Itsekiri* traders' meagre gift, ordered a total cessation of the supply of oil palm produce to them. To ensure a strict compliance with his directives and discourage smuggling he placed a 'curse' on the sale and supply of the commodity to *Itsekiri* traders. The 'curse' meant trade on the commodity became a capital offence and consequently, all transactions with *Itsekiri* traders ceased. The effect was devastating, and trade was at a standstill on the Benin River. The *Itsekiri* traders urged by their European financiers quickly sent the messenger back to Benin with tributes worth about eighty-pounds sterling (£80), which they considered adequate to persuade the Omo N'Oba to lift the prohibition, and also grant permission to establish more trading stations.

Although the European traders would later claim that the Omo N'Oba had stopped trade intermittently to extort more tributes from the *Itsekiri* traders, they knew the £80 gift would not persuade the Omo N'Oba to grant their desires because he was not interested in the oil palm produce trade with *Itsekiri* traders. And even before the *Itsekiri* messenger came back from Benin City, the traders decided to call on the Niger Coast Protectorate to help them to 'open up' Benin territory, which was in plain terms the removal of the Benin king from the scene. Consequently, a petition (dated April 13, 1896) was forwarded to Major Peter Copland-Crawford, the Vice-Consul of the District, for onward transmission to the Consul-General. The petition was signed by Edward Straw, the agent for Messrs African Association Limited, J.H. Swainson, the agent for Mr James Pinnock, G.J. Greenshields, the agent for Messrs A. Miller Brothers and Company, and Otto Bauer, the agent for Messer Bey and Zimmer. And it read:

Sir,

We, the European Traders in Benin River beg to draw your attention to a matter, which is of the first importance to us as Traders. The King of Benin has again stopped trade without any apparent cause or grievance against the middleman. On a suggestion of the Consul General the Chiefs in the River sent a representative to the king to pay their respects to him, and to further propitiate him, so that he would allow his people to continue trading freely, as they have been doing recently. They sent him a present of goods to the value of forty pounds sterling. When the representative got halfway to the City, he was met by the King's people, who would not allow him to proceed, as the presents were insufficient.

The representative returned to the River and reported this to the Chiefs, who were then compelled to increase the value of their present, this they did to the extent of another forty pounds sterling. The representative has again proceeded to the City; he has not yet returned.

This month and the following three months being the "Oil Season" months the fact of the King's arbitrary commands to his people not to obtain or sell produce to the middlemen will at once make itself apparent to you, that this is a very serious matter indeed to us in Benin River, who are now wholly dependent for the trade, on which comes from the king's Country. Even should the king open trade on the receipt of the aforementioned percent; we wish to point out to you that he may again stop trade for no other reason than to extort money from the middlemen.

We wish further to draw your attention to the fact, that on any native going from the River to trade at any of the King's markets, he has, previous to buying any produce, to send a present to the King for this privilege. We are aware that this is the custom of this Country, but in this particular portion of your district, the natives are further frequently called upon to make other presents, and in the event of their not complying their trade is at once stopped. We would respectfully request you to forward this letter, or a copy of same with your remarks on the subject to the Consul General.

We are sending a copy to our respective firms.

This petition is confirmed by the Niger Coast Protectorate official dispatch CSO 3/3/3, p. 262 of April 13 1896 report, European traders in Benin to Major Copland-Crawford. Reporting the stoppage of trade by the Benin King.

There is no way to know if the Omo N'Oba would have lifted the embargo or allowed the establishment of more trading settlements because at the time in question the Benin Kingdom was faced with a serious threat in her eastern province. The *Eka* people of Agbor, a town about 80 kilometres east of Benin City, goaded by agents of the Royal Niger Company, had stopped paying tributes to Benin kingdom and were virtually on the verge of rebellion. Hence the demands by a few *Itsekiri* traders for a resumption of trade were considered insignificant as preparations were being made to contain the more serious and tangible threat. Omo N'Oba Ovonramwen ordered the establishment of a military garrison at Obadan, a town about 40 kilometres from Benin City and a few kilometres Northwest of Agbor, for the recruitment and training of conscripts, to crush the rebellion. The *Itsekiri* traders who were much aware of the crisis accepted the trade embargo as temporary and decided to wait and 'sit down' until the *Eka* problem was resolved. On the contrary, the Europeans traders, who had become much more aware of Benin kingdom's economic potentials, especially in rubber and timber, were now much determined to wrestle control of trade in Benin kingdom from Omo N'Oba Ovonramwen. Consequently, in June 1886, the principal agent of African Association Limited sent a memo to his company stating: 'there is an immediate prospect of large returns from trade within Benin territory immediately the Protectorate take steps to "open up" Benin territory'. The report was intended to urge his company to exert more political pressure on Whitehall to grant Niger Coast Protectorate permission to invade Benin kingdom.

Then towards the last days of October 1896, an *Itsekiri* delegation, which was led by Itsie, an Itsekiri prince, and included Chiefs Dogho and Dudu, the two leading Itsekiri traders, came to Benin City to resolve a long-standing communal matter. The mission primary purpose was to implore Omo N'Oba Ovonramwen to revoke the curse Omo N'Oba Osemwende had placed on Olu Akengbuwa and the Itsekiri royal family. However, Chiefs Dogho and Dudu were on a quite different mission. They came to Benin City primarily on the orders of their European financiers to discuss how to resolve the oil palm trade embargo, and also ask the Omo N'Oba if he would allow a Niger Coast Protectorate official to visit Benin City. The Omo N'Oba in his talks with the Chiefs demanded 1000 bundles of corrugated iron roofing sheets as a pre-condition for the resumption of trade. He then informed them that a decision on whether or not to allow a visit to Benin City by a Niger Coast Protectorate official would be made at the end of the *Ihiekhu* ceremonies, the Edo Thanksgiving rituals, which mark the end of the Edo calendar year, that is, February 1897.

On October 31, 1896, incidentally, the very day the *Itsekiri* trading Chiefs arrived from Benin City, the acting Commissioner and Consul General of the Protectorate, Mr James Robert Phillips (Major Ralph Moor was on leave) arrived in Sapele apparently in response to the European traders' petitions. During the discussions, the trading agents, true to the long-established European tradition of dishonesty in their dealings with any indigenous people whose economy they want to destroy and the lands they intend to violently acquire, told Phillips the tale he desired to hear. And which was that the Benin king was crucifying slaves, disrupting trade in the region, and blackmailing and extorting tributes from the Itsekiri people. They further told Phillips that the Benin king had refused to give a definite reply to their request (allowing a Protectorate's official to visit Benin City) because the king wanted to extort more tributes from their *Itsekiri* trading partners. At the end of the talks the chief agent of African Association Limited, made available to the acting Consul-General an 'intelligence report' (a top-secret memo that was intended only for the company's management) on Benin kingdom's economic potentials which stated, 'there is a future before the Benin River'. Phillips concurred with the traders' argument that the only way the Protectorate and the British traders could achieve a complete political and economic control of the region was ousting the Benin king. In his meeting with Chiefs Dogho and Dudu, Phillips ordered the *Itsekiri* chiefs not to supply iron roofing sheets to the Benin king, and also stop paying tributes to him.

On his return to Old Calabar, armed with the needed pretext to "open the roads" and also "transport the petty king of Benin and his Juju men, somewhere else" as envisaged by Mr James Pinnock, Phillips began preparations for the anticipated early 1897 invasion of Benin City. After completing all formalities for the operation, he made a formal request to the Foreign Office for approval. In his request dated November 16, 1896, and addressed to the Under Secretary of State, Phillips wrote:

Sir,

I have the honour to state for the information of the Marques of Salisbury that I visited the Benin district shortly after my arrival in the Protectorate, and, on the 31st October in company with Captain Gallway and Mr. Locks, the Acting Vice-Consul of that Division, held a long consultation with the Jakri Chiefs and the Agents of the various trading firms established on the river, from whom I obtained a very clear idea of the state of affairs now prevailing in that part of the Protectorate in which Benin City is situated.

2. As you are doubtless aware, the Jakris (*Itsekiri*) are a tribe of "middlemen" traders who try to make their living by trading in this district between the Benin people and the European traders established on the river.

3. I have carefully read the following despatches bearing on the subject which I now propose dealing with to which I beg to refer, viz.: Sir Claude MacDonald's despatch No. 26 to the Foreign Office of 26th May 1892. Mr. Moor's despatches to the Foreign Office, Nos. 39 and 58 of 12th September 1895 and 18th July 1896 respectively. I have also, of course, discussed the matter in all its bearings with Captain Gallway, who visited Benin City and succeeded in making a treaty with the King in March 1892.

4. Benin City is situated forty-five miles from the Protectorate station of Benin on the river. It is approached in a general direction of East-North East from the riverside by a creek providing a water-way for lighters, surf-boats, or launches, for 20 miles up to the village of Gwato inhabited, by friendly people - from this village a path through the forest leads to the first clearing immediately in front of the City itself, a distance of twenty five miles as measured by Captain Gallway by pedometer. The few small villages, which lie at rare intervals on either side of the path, are inhabited by harmless and inoffensive people. The city is also approachable from the frontiers of the Colony of Lagos by roads, which are described by Major Ewart the Travelling Commissioner employed by that Government in general terms as "good" - a distance of some 40 miles. It is described by Captain Gallway as a straggling town not very thickly populated and having no defences except the mud

walls which surround the various compounds of which the city consists. The surrounding country is fertile, and according to the accounts of those who have been there, is teeming with valuable products, especially Palm Kernels. There is nothing in the shape of a standing army in the country and the inhabitants appear to be, if not a peace-loving, at any rate a most unwarlike people, whose only exploits during many generations have been an occasional quarrel with their neighbours about trade or slave-raiding, and it appears at least improbable that they have any arms to speak of except the usual number of trade guns to be found among all the tribes of West Africa. When Captain Gallway visited the city, the only canon he saw were half a dozen old Portuguese guns; they were lying in the grass unmounted there is no reason to think that they are not anxious to collect the kernels and other produce with which the country abounds, and the Jakris are of course eager to convey the produce to the factories, and have spent much money in their efforts to gain open markets.

5. The King of Benin City is not a man of war but a "Fetish" "Priest-king", deriving all the power he has from the superstitions fear which his people have for the King's "Juju." He lives in retirement in the city, for the most part invisible to his people hiding in his house and continually issuing his edicts putting "Juju" on various products extorting presents from the Jakris by making promises, which he never carries out, and persecuting his own people with despotic and cruel laws. From what the Jakri Chiefs told me I have no doubt that human sacrifices are carried out by the King from time to time and executions (so called) are very common. The latter take the form of crucifixions, abundant evidence of which Captain Gallway himself saw in 1892 and described in his report of the 30th March 1892, to which I beg to call attention.

6. In March 1892 a Treaty was made with the King by Captain Gallway on behalf of this Government in which the King undertook to protect trade. He also promised Captain Gallway on that occasion to open up the kernel and gum copal trade. In spite of this the king has continued ever since to do everything in his power to stop his people from trading and prevent the Government from opening up the country. By means of his Fetish he has succeeded in a marked degree. He has permanently placed a 'Juju" on kernels, the most profitable product of the country, and the penalty for trading in this produce is death. He has closed the market and has only occasionally consented to open them in certain places on receipt of presents from the

Jakri Chiefs, only however, to close them again when he desires more blackmail.

7. After the signing of the treaty an intermittent trade was kept up by means of constant presents being given to the King by the Jakri middlemen but it was constantly interrupted and the King, or rather the "Fetish man" has never taken his "Juju" off kernels.

8. A climax was reached on the 2nd April 1896 when the King deliberately stopped all his people from trading. By order of the Consul General pacific means were at once taken to open up trade again. A deputation from Jakri Chiefs was sent up to propitiate the King by the usual present, on this occasion one of £40 in value. This was contemptuously refused as insufficient. It was then doubled and accepted by the King who promised in return to open five markets. Up to the date of my visit to Benin River, these markets had not been opened. A Lagos man trading in the Protectorate also went to the king by the advice of Mr. Moor, chiefly with a view to asking the king to start the "rubber" industry, the country abounding in that product. He made presents to the King to the value of over £30, but the results of his mission have been nil. The King has now asked for 1,000 sheets of corrugated iron to build a house with before he will accede to the demands made. The Jakri Chiefs promised to give the iron directly the markets were opened, and at the same time asked the King to receive a Government officer. His reply was that he was making a big Custom to last four months and could not do so until it was over. Besides acceding to the "blackmailing" demands of this Fetish-Priest, which I have described, the Jakri Chiefs have, according to custom, sent presents to all the markets and in individual cases numerous presents have been made to the king whenever native custom demanded it.

9. From what I have stated in the preceding paragraph the Marques of Salisbury will, I think, be assured that His Lordship's instructions to deal with this matter by pacific means have been literally obeyed and have failed to produce the results desired. I felt so convinced that every means had been un-successfully tried that I have advised the Jakri Chiefs to discontinue their presents and not to send the thousand sheets of iron. It is true that this action brings matters to a climax, but I do not think that I should have done my duty if I had countenanced any more what has been proved to be nothing but blackmailing.

10. The result of the action of the King is this the Jakri Chiefs, great traders as they are to use their own expressive words 'sitting down'. There are no markets open - until a few weeks ago there was a small market at a place

called Ekiti, but now even that is closed. The Jakris have invested their money in trying to open trade with no return, and "The African Association" and other trading firms on the river are doing no trade because they are now, according to a petition addressed to the Vice Consul of the Division and signed by the Agents of all the firms on the river on the 13th April last, "wholly dependent for their trade on what comes down from the King's country". This of course refers to the traders the Lower River, as Sapele is not affected to such an extent. I attach a copy of this petition, in short the trade of the river, which is capable of giving very large returns to natives, European traders and to Her majesty's Government, is at a standstill while the produce lies rotting in the forests, all because of the malpractices of a man whose only power consists of the awe he inspires by his "Fetish" reputation.

11. It is difficult to submit for His Lordship's information, statistics of the trade which will give a true idea of the effect of this stoppage of trade, because I have no means of separating the returns of revenue for this district from those of other district of the river, The following facts, however are most significant: Chief Dore, an individual Jakri trader, stated that in 1891-2 he obtained 250 puncheons in twelve months and that this was his usual year's trade, while during the twelve months previous to the Broheimie Expedition, he only got 25 puncheons, and now he is getting none (I mention the Broheimie Expedition because what Chief Dore states shows that his trade has been paralysed before that Expedition took place). Mr. Whitehead, Agent of the African Association informed me that in 1890-93 the monthly supply brought to the firm's factory averaged 90 puncheons from all sources while latterly they have not received more than thirty per month and during October last he had not seen a single puncheon brought down from the Benin country.

12. I have now before me a copy of a letter addressed to the African Association Limited the chief trading firm in the Benin River by their head agent there, which when it has written was not intended to be read by any representative of Her Majesty's Government. Its object is to impress upon the firm that the writer is assured of the fact that there is an immediate prospect of large returns from trade with the Benin country in the very near future, that is, immediately the Government take steps to open up the country, and it expresses a firm conviction that the desired end will shortly be accomplished and an option based on personal observation that "there is a future before the Benin River"

13. To sum up, the situation in this: The King of Benin whose country is within a British Protectorate and whose city lies within fifty miles of a protectorate Customs Station and who has signed a Treaty with Her Majesty's representative has deliberately stopped all trade and effectually blocked the way to all progress in that part of the protectorate. The Jakri traders, a most important and most loyal tribe, whose prosperity depends to a very great extent upon the produce they can get from the Benin country, have appealed to this Government to give them such assistance as will enable them to pursue their lawful trade. The whole of the English merchants represented on the river have petitioned the Government for aid to enable them to keep their factories open, and last but not perhaps least, the revenues of this Protectorate are suffering.

14. I am certain that there is only one remedy that is to depose the King of Benin from his Stool. I am convinced from information which leaves no room for doubt, as well as from experience of native character, that pacific measures are now quite useless and that the time has now come to remove the obstruction.

15. I therefore ask His Lordship's permission to visit Benin City in February next, to depose and remove the King of Benin and to establish Native Council in his place, and take such further steps for the opening up of the country as the occasion may require I do not anticipate any serious resistance from the people of the country there is every reason to believe that they would be glad to get rid of their King but in order to obviate any danger I wish to take up a sufficient armed force consisting of 250 troops, 2 pounder guns, a Maxim and 1 Rocket apparatus of the Niger Coast Protectorate Force and a detachment of Lagos Hausas 150 strong, if His Lordship and the Secretary of State for the Colonies will sanction the use of Colonial Forces to this extent.

16. I am fully aware of the responsibility I am incurring in recommending this course, but I have no hesitation in asking His Lordship to impose confidence to this extent in myself and the tried Officers serving in this Protectorate. I respectfully submit that the arrangements necessary to effect the deposition of the King may be left to myself and staff. All calculations as to ammunition, supplies, rations, &c., have been already made. Should His Lordship give his sanction to my proposal I request that a cablegram may be sent to me directly this despatch has been dealt with, which I ask may be done as soon us possible, to enable me to make all arrangements for transport, porters, water and other necessaries and to start early in February.

And also that a Cable may be sent to the Lagos Government authorising the Inspector General of Constabulary to proceed to Old Calabar to consult with this Government at once

17. Mr. Moor, who is of course fully cognizant of all matters dealt with in this despatch will doubtless be consulted by His Lordship, and in conclusion. I have the honour to state that everything I have stated is subject to Mr. Moor's approval

Postscript

I would add that I have reason to hope that sufficient ivory may be found in the King's house to pay the expenses incurred in removing the King from his Stool.

This letter is confirmed by the November 17, 1896 Niger Coast Protectorate official dispatch CSO 3/3/3, p. 240 report; J.R. Phillips to Foreign Office. Advising the deposition of the Benin King.

Phillips' proposals that were based on its economic and 'humanitarian' considerations were convincing enough to get the prompt response of the Foreign Office. Consequently, a 'pressing' letter was forwarded to the undersecretary of the Colonial Office for further deliberation. The letter dated December 24, 1896, and signed by Mr Francis Bertie of the Foreign Office, read:

Sir,

I am directed by the Marquis of Salisbury to transmit to you a copy of a despatch from Her Majesty's Acting Commissioner and Consul General in the Niger Coast Protectorate recommending the deposition of the King of Benin on the ground that he obstructs trade against the wishes of his own people and continues inhuman practices. It will be seen that Mr. Phillips proposes that the expedition which would go up to Benin should consist of 250 men of the Protectorate forces and 150 men of the Colonial Forces of Lagos, and that he anticipates little or no resistance. Lord Salisbury would be glad to be favoured with any observations, which Mr. Secretary Chamberlain may wish to offer on this despatch. I am to request that the answer to my present letter may be sent with as little delay as possible, because, if the expedition is sanctioned the necessary preliminary arrangements must be completed so as to allow it to start early in February. I am to add that the Intelligence Division of the War Office are being consulted on the military aspect of Mr. Phillips proposal.

On January 4, 1897, a response, with reference number 26459/96, to the 'pressing' letter was signed by Mr John Bramston of the Colonial Office and it read:

Sir,

I am directed by Mr. Secretary Chamberlain to state, for the information of the Marques of Salisbury in reply to your letter of the 24th of December, that he concurs in the proposals made by Her Majesty's Commissioner and Consul General in the Niger Coast Protectorate for the deposition of the King of Benin and that he will instruct the Officer Administering the Government of Lagos to render Mr. Phillips such assistance as he can with regard to the contemplated expedition.

2. It must, however, be remembered that the attitude of Ilorin requires constant vigilance on the part of the Lagos Government, and that in view of the consequent, demands upon the small armed force at his disposal it may not be possible for Captain Denton to spare a detachment of 150 Hausas with due regard to the interests of the Colony.

3. I am to enclose a copy of a telegram, which has been addressed to Captain Denton on the subject.

Major Moor, who was on holiday in England, was consulted on his deputy's intentions, and Moor readily endorsed it. He even suggested that a gunboat and a British Navy Royal Marine unit should reinforce the proposed expedition. For one reason or another the Colonial Secretary was not willing to release troops for the proposed expedition but nonetheless on 5th January 1897 a dispatch, which was signed by Mr. J. Chamberlain of the Foreign Office, was sent to the Government of Lagos Colony asking Captain Denton if he could render any assistance to Phillips' undertaking. And the message was:

Sir,

I have the honour to transmit to you, with reference to my telegram of the 2nd instant the accompanying copy of a correspondence respecting the proposed expedition against the king of Benin.

However, by the time this telegram, and another one of January 8, 1897, instructing Phillips to postpone his proposed invasion for at least a year, because the 400 men deemed adequate for the operation could not be provided, were dispatched, the acting Commissioner and Consul-General of the Niger Coast Protectorate was already dead.

UGBINE: JANUARY 4, 1897

'... the white man is bringing war' - Itsekiri courier to Benin City. January 3, 1897.
'No Revolvers, gentlemen!' - Mr James Robert Philip, acting Consul General, Niger Coast Protectorate. January 4, 1897.

On December 27, 1896, Mr James Robert Phillips, acting Commissioner and Consul-General, Niger Coast Protectorate, accompanied by Captain Alan Maxwell Boisragon, Commandant Niger Coast Protectorate Force, and Captains Searle and Ringer, also of the Niger Coast Protectorate Force, left Old Calabar for Sapele. While Captains Searle and Ringer were on 'Punitive Expedition' to loot and burn down some Isoko towns and settlements, acting Consul-General Phillips and Captain Boisragon, were on a clandestine and unauthorised mission to Benin City to abduct the Benin king and steal his 'ivory' to pay for the venture.

Why Phillips embarked on the mission, which he had himself proposed for February 1897, without waiting for approval from the Foreign Office, is subject to speculations. The author of a famous book on Benin claimed that Phillips was 'ill advised'. One expert of African art history argued that Phillips was 'obstinate', while an eminent scholar of African history maintained that Phillips was 'inexperienced and naive'. It is quite likely Phillips' decision to embark on the expedition was a fatal error of judgement that stemmed from flawed intelligence reports, which claimed that Benin kingdom had no effective armed force. It is also possible that the acting Consul-General wanted to perform a daring feat that would have conceivably engraved his name in the pages of British Colonial history. However, two writers, R. S. Billett, and W.N.M. Geary believe somehow Phillips became aware that the Foreign Office was unwilling to approve or unable to secure the extra troops needed for his proposed invasion of Benin City, and thus recommended that the invasion be put on hold for at least a year. While R. S. Billett, in his tribute to Captain Claude William Robertson (Royal Marine Light Infantry) who took part in the 'Benin Punitive Expedition', argued that Phillips embarked on his clandestine mission to make a name for himself, W.N.M. Geary, in his book, *Nigeria Under British Rule*, believed that Philip was a courageous and high-minded British official, who was determined to follow the 'course of duty', and redeem the protectorate's image that had been dented by the hasty retreats of Protectorate forces whenever they had been confronted by Benin border guards in previous intrusions into Benin territories, which the writer termed 'an injury to the prestige of the Protectorate'. Also in an article, 'The Looting of Nigerian Art', by Becky Ceravolo, the writer concludes, 'In retrospect, it can be speculated that the (Phillips) reaction was either one of misplaced superiority or plain egoism'. Whatever were Phillips' reasons, for his arrogance and imprudence, he met the fate reserved for the misguided zealot, and befittingly his name would be consigned to a few lines in the pages of British Colonial history. There is little doubt that had the acting Commissioner and Consul-General of the Niger Coast Protectorate survived the Ugbine military disaster his career would have ended in disgrace. No wonder when his clandestine invasion force was caught up in the Benin militia's ambush, Phillips probably realised the enormity of his folly and hence quietly resigned himself to his fate. 'No revolvers, gentlemen!' he is quoted to have said.

When the Niger Coast Protectorate Force units arrived in Sapele on January 1, 1897, Chiefs Dogho and Dudu were highly agitated because it was very obvious Phillips' mission to Benin City was not a "friendly" or trade visit, and hence they tried to dissuade the acting Consul-General not to press forward to Benin City because they were convinced that the mission would end in disaster. According to one writer, 'A local Itsekiri Chief, Dogho, advised Phillips it would be suicide to proceed'. And in one other publication it is claimed, 'Chief Dudu warned that the Benin king was making "country custom" and he would not allow any white man to enter the city'. Undeniably, blinded by the quest for glory or 'call of duty', the acting Consul-General brushed aside the warnings but to avoid undue suspicion on the way to Benin City he ordered the Niger Coast Protectorate Force's Drum and Fife band to remain behind in Sapele. And then the revolvers of the British officers as well as the repeater rifles of the Niger Coast Protectorate Force African soldiers were carefully concealed in the head packs of the African soldiers who were then disguised as porters. Unfortunately for Phillips, that same evening one Itsekiri Chief sent a messenger to Benin City and inform Omo N'Oba Ovonramwen: 'the white man is bringing war'.

In the Benin king's palace, the ague ceremony was being observed. Ague is a Christian derived abstinence and fasting festival that was instituted by Omo N'Oba Esigie (r. c. 1504-1530). And because the rituals are aimed at the spiritual renewal and strengthening of the participants, they refrain from all worldly pleasures. In addition, they were duty-bound to avoid contact with visitors, intimate contact with women and drinking of intoxicating beverages. The disturbing message brought by the Itsekiri messenger compelled the

Omo N'Oba to break with tradition, and summon the city's nobles and high-ranking *Ekhaemwen* (titled spokesmen. sing. *Okhaemwen*, titled spokesman) for consultations. He refused to believe that the white men, whom he assumed were his 'friends', and had no quarrel with whatsoever, were coming to Benin City with hostile intentions. He was of the view the white men were probably coming on a 'friendly' visit hence he argued they should be allowed a safe passage into the city to determine whether the visit was a friendly or hostile one. His contention was supported by most of the elderly *Ekhaemwen*, who argued that although Mr McTaggart had entered the city, some years earlier, unannounced and uninvited with a large armed escort, his visit turned out to be a 'friendly' one. On the contrary Okizi, the *Iyase*, Benin kingdom's principal *Okhaemwen* and supreme commander of the Benin Army, supported by his powerful army commanders, was convinced that the *Itsekiri* warning was genuine, chiefly because in the past two years the kingdom's border guards had on several occasions discouraged attempts by the Niger Coast Protectorate Force to forcibly enter Benin territories. Actually, at the particular time, a number of suspected spies (some Krumen from Sierra Leone and others from the British colony of Lagos) were in detention in the city. The men were captured inside Benin territories in late November 1896, and although they claimed to be rubber collectors, they had sophisticated firearms (revolvers) in their possessions.

The *Iyase* was convinced the 'white man was bringing war', and he countered the Omo N'Oba's argument by making references to the fate of Nana Olumo, who had also considered himself to be a 'friend' of the white man. Nonetheless, at the end of the meeting, no concrete decision was achieved but it was quite obvious the *Iyase* was determined to kill the intruding white men. Since there were no soldiers stationed in the city (most of them were stationed at Obadan training camp, and other border outposts and military garrisons in the kingdom) Okizi ordered all *Ekhaemwen* to provide personnel for a task force. Most of the younger *Ekhaemwen*, notably the *Aiyobahan*, *Ehondor*, *Ehanire*, *Ihaza*, *Inneh*, *Obaseki*, *Obanor*, and *Osague* made available some of their personal retainers and servants for the task force. *Okhaemwen* Irabor, the *Ologbose*, a hereditary senior field commander of the Benin Army, was appointed to lead the task force, with a warning from *Iyase* Okizi not to allow any white man set foot in the City or else he (Irabor) would pay dearly for it. Later in the day when the Omo N'Oba became aware Okizi had sent a task force to wipe out the intruders, he sent a formal message to the *Iyase* entreating him to enjoin the task force commanders not to kill the white men but grant them a safe passage into Benin City. Unfortunately, the task force commanders and their militia were already on the road to Ugbine to fulfil their destinies and that of the ancient city of Benin.

On January 2 1897, Mr. James Robert Phillips, Major Peter Copland-Crawford, Captain Alan Maxwell Boisragon, Captain Arthur I. Maling, and Mr. Ralph F. Locke, including Mr. Kenneth Campbell, a District Commissioner, Dr. Robert H. Elliott, a medical doctor, Mr. Harry S. Powis, an agent of Messrs Miller Brothers trading company, Mr. Thomas Gordon, an agent of Africa Association, and Mr. Hubert Clarke, an interpreter of mixed race, escorted by 250 African soldiers of the Niger Coast Protectorate Force set out for Benin City. This extraordinary expedition, the first and probably the only one of its kind in British colonial history, was an abduction and armed robbery mission, which was to be paid for by the victim's treasures. On January 3, 1897, the expedition arrived in Gwato, and the *ohen olokun, Olokun* priest, and headman of the town, assuming the intruders were on a trade mission formally received them, by ordering the washing of the British officers and traders feet. The washing of European visitors' feet was introduced in the 16th century by Omo N'Oba Esigie. It was a sort of quarantine practice aimed at preventing Europeans visitors from contaminating the soil of Benin kingdom and thus bringing disease and harm to the Edo people. The British officers and trading agents were apparently satisfied their deception had paid off, consequently they spent the day leisurely taking photographs as if they were on a picnic trip. The next day, January 4, 1897, escorted by two guides the Olokun priest had provided, the invasion force embarked on the final leg of its mission. Since Phillips was not expecting any armed resistance, he declined to issue orders to carry arms for any contingency and thus the revolvers and repeater rifles remained locked up, and the machetes remained tied to the head packs of the African soldiers.

Meanwhile, the Benin militia, whose number had swollen to several hundred, set up an ambush on the outskirts of Ugbine village. When Phillips and his intruders walked into the ambush the militia commanders restrained their men from attacking. They wanted to ascertain whether the intruders' intentions were hostile or friendly. It became apparent that the number of African porters accompanying the white nine men was too many for a 'friendly visit', and worse still all the porters had machetes tied to their head packs. In practice, one white man was usually accompanied by seven African porters with only one or two of them carrying a machete. It was the large number of porters with machetes tied to the porters head packs that alarmed the Benin militia commanders, which undeniably strengthened their suspicions that the white men were not on a 'friendly' visit. Indeed as noted by a publication, 'the mission was too large for a peaceful purpose and too small for defence in case of need'. The Benin militia commanders convinced that the white men were on a hostile mission, decided to first attack the porters, whom they considered armed because of the machetes tied to their head packs. This was catastrophic for the British officers because their revolvers were locked up in the head packs, and consequently (except Alan Boisragon and Ralph Locke who managed to escape with some of the African troopers) they, including the two trading agents and many of the Niger Coast Protectorate soldiers, were all shot or cut down unarmed.

The Benin militia retrieved the British officers' revolvers, the repeater rifles and other belongings from the African troopers' head packs, and late in the evening of that day danced triumphantly into Benin City with their trophies and spoils of war.

The Omo N'Oba was upset when the commanders arrived in the palace with the war trophies, captives, and other enemy's belongings because he was convinced the Ugbine battle would bring disaster to Benin City. The commanders, flushed with success, were confident the white man's threat had been resolved once and for all. Omo N'Oba Ovonramwen was however not convinced. And when he turned to his most senior war chieftains, the Iyase, and Ezomo, for military preparations against any anticipated British counter-attack he was disappointed. Iyase Okizi, chief war commander of the Benin Army, who had ordered the destruction of the British intruders, for reasons best known to him, chose to distance himself from any preparations for war. And his deputy, Ezomo Osarogiagbon, quietly withdrew to his Uzebu domain. Also alarming, the other senior war chieftains could not agree on how to tackle the problem. Hence, Omo N'Oba Ovonramwen was compelled to turn to the palace priests and medicine men for alternative solutions. Sadly the palace priests and medicine men embarked on the largest scale of human sacrifices hitherto unknown in the history of Benin. And the exercise, which persisted nearly until the moment Benin City was captured, was to give Benin City the infamous name: The 'City of Blood'.

BENIN CITY: THE SACK THAT WAS

BENIN CITY: THE SACK THAT WAS

'We went out to burn down the Queens Palace and our bluejackets went out and burned down the King's Palace.' - Trooper Lucy of the H.M.S. Theseus.
'... a curious brass jug... I obtained out of the wall at the back of the king's compound.' - Dr. Felix Roth, British Surgeon.

Mr Ralph Locke, Captain Alan Boisragon and the few African soldiers who survived the Ugbine ambush eventually arrived in Sapele on January 9, 1897, and immediately a telegram was dispatched to the Colony of Lagos informing the administration of acting Consul-General Phillips expedition disaster. The following day, January 10, 1897, another telegram was sent out from Lagos to the British Foreign Office in London. This was the message that began the distortion of the events that led to the annihilation of Captain Boisragon's Niger Coast Protectorate unit at Ugbine, which in turn, to a very large extent, led to the massive distortion of much of Benin kingdom's history, and the misinterpretation of her artworks by scholars and experts of African art history and history.

The British Government's response was swift but the British army, citing financial and logistic problems, was reluctant to engage in an immediate campaign against Benin kingdom. However the British Navy accepted the mission, and on January 12, 1897, Rear-Admiral Harry Rawson, commanding the British Navy Squadron at the Cape of Good Hope, was appointed by the British Admiralty to lead an expedition to capture the Benin king and destroy Benin City. The Rear Admiral assured the Admiralty that it would take him about six weeks and about fifty thousand pounds (£50,000) to accomplish the task. Consul-General Ralph Moor then hurried back from England to Old Calabar and formally declared war on the Benin Kingdom. Phillips' death had made it possible for Moor to fulfil his desires and those of the European trading companies. The man who sowed death and destruction in the settlements, towns, and city-states of the Niger Delta, and played a leading role in the events that led to the destruction of Phillips invasion force, with a tongue in the cheek christened the mission, 'Benin Punitive Expedition'. It was a fitting tribute to a lie: a lie, which was to be ardently maintained up until the present time by 'eminent' writers, art historians and historians, including mainstream publications, that the 'Benin Punitive Expedition' was a reprisal for the killing of seven unarmed British envoys and traders on a peaceful diplomatic mission by a group of fetish and savage Benin chiefs, which they christened 'Benin Massacre'.

In the last week of January 1897, Rear-Admiral Harry Rawson deployed the H.M.S. *St George*, *Theseus*, *Forte* and *Philomel* with about 900 sailors to the Bight of Benin Also deployed were the H.M.S. *Phoebe*, *Widgeon*, *Magpie*, *Barossa* and *Alecto* and an additional 300 Royal Marines brought from England with the hospital ship *Malacca*. The invasion force was reinforced by some 250 African soldiers of the Niger Coast Protectorate Force. On February 7, 1897, the Rear Admiral summoned all the Itsekiri trading chiefs in the Benin River region to Sapele and informed them of the retribution that he was about to mete out on Benin kingdom for the 'massacre' of seven white chiefs. The Itsekiri chiefs were told, '... the Benin king and his "Juju" priests will be killed, and the Benin "Juju" houses will be burned so that the power of the Benin "Juju" will be forever broken'.

On February 9, the British Navy assault on Benin kingdom began, and the expedition's field commanders were given explicit orders by Rear-Admiral Harry Rawson to burn down all Benin kingdom's towns and villages, and hang the Benin king wherever and whenever he was captured. The invasion force was composed of three columns: the Sapoba, Gwato and Main Columns. The Sapoba Column, consisting of Royal Marines and sailors of the H.M.S. *Phoebe*, *Alecto* and *Magpie* was deployed to Benin kingdom's southwestern flank. The Column was charged with the destruction of Sokponba village on the Igbaghon (Jamieson) River, outflanking the defending Benin army and preventing Benin people from escaping into the neighbouring areas. The Gwato Column, made up of about 100 Royal Marines and sailors of the H.M.S. *Philomel*, *Widgeon*, and *Barossa*, was charged with blockading the Benin River, engaging the Benin soldiers defending the Gwato/Benin City road and the destruction of all Benin towns and villages from Gwato up to the river port of Ikoro. The Main Column, consisted of 120 British marines, 100 British sailors of the H.M.S. *Theseus* and *Forte* and 30 African scouts, was supported by 250 Africans troops of the Niger Coast Protectorate Force. The Column was charged with the destruction of all Benin towns and settlements from Ologbo to Benin City.

The Sapoba Column, commanded by Captain McGills, sailed from Sapele through the Igbaghon River towards Sokponba village, and on February 11, after a heavy bombardment, the invaders successfully occupied the settlement. Although there was little resistance by Benin defenders especially because the settlement had a large Itsekiri population, the settlement was razed. The invaders moved forward but a few kilometres north of the settlement, a Benin militia led by *Okakuo* (Commander) Izibiri stopped the Column's progress. The invaders quickly erected a defensive stockade and held out against the Benin militia attacks. Eventually on February 20, after incurring severe losses, including Lieutenant Commander Pritchard of the H.M.S. *Alecto*, the invaders abandoned the stockade, and withdrew with their dead and wounded to Ughareki, near Sapele.

On the same February 9th the Gwato Column, commanded by Captain O'Callaghan sailed up the Benin River onward to Gwato. The invaders occupied and burnt down Gele-Gele settlement on the Benin River, and the next day, February 10, 1897, the column moved on to Gwato. After an extensive bombardment, the British sailors and Royal Marines landed and tried to occupy the town but the invaders were unaware that Gwato was Benin's major port and gateway to the 'European world', and hence it was the most heavily defended Benin position. The invaders encountered a very determined and stiff resistance mounted by Benin and *Igbile* cult militias commanded by *Okakuo* Ebeikhinmwin. And after a bitter and bloody battle in the town's main square, the British forces withdrew back to Gele-Gele with their wounded, which included Captain O'Callaghan and Lieutenant Commander Hunt of the *Widgeon*. On the February 14, again the invaders launched a fresh attack on Gwato and tried to occupy the town but were held back on the outskirts of the town until February 25, 1897, when they were eventually relieved by a detachment of Niger Coast Protectorate Force commanded by Captain Henry Gallwey. Thereafter the town was looted and burnt down even though no resistance was encountered. Some of the town's artefacts including *Igbile* cult masks can be seen today in some British museums. Meanwhile, on February 12, 1897, the Main Column, commanded by Lieutenant Colonel Bruce Hamilton, began its assault on Benin kingdom. Ologbo was heavily shelled and the British Marines and sailors crossed the river with boats and tugs provided by the European traders and their Itsekiri partners. The Benin defenders commanded by *Okakuo* Urugbusi were forced to withdraw since their ancient flintlocks were no match for the invaders' superior Maxim guns, seven-pounder guns, and rockets tubes. Later in the day the settlement was occupied, razed and thereafter a field hospital was erected in its ruins. The next day supported by its formidable arsenal the column moved forward toward Benin City. Although the five-kilometre long column was continually harassed by Benin defenders, but backed by Maxims, Seven-pounder guns, and the resolute African soldiers, who bore the brunt of the fighting, the Main Column pressed on relentlessly toward its objective adhering strictly to Rear Admiral Harry Rawson's directives. Accordingly, all towns, villages, and settlements such as Obaretin, Obayantor, and Oko to mention a few that were on Column's path were completely razed. On the February 18, shortly after leaving Oko, a settlement a few kilometres south of Benin City, the Column was struck in the rear by Benin defenders armed with repeater rifles. The invaders suffered heavy casualties but a reinforcement unit equipped with Maxim and seven-pounder guns quickly routed the belated counter-attack. The next morning February 19, the advance guard of the Main Column entered the city through Unueru quarter, about a kilometre southeast of the king's palace. They were held back briefly by a group of Benin irregulars, armed with repeater rifles, led by Asoro, an *Omuada*, (ceremonial sword-bearer). And here once again the invaders suffered heavy casualties, including Captain Byrne of the Royal Marine Light Infantry and Dr Fyfe, one of the Column's medical doctor, by late afternoon apart from some sporadic gunfire, the men and officers of the Main Column occupied the Benin king's palace ground, the royal quarters and much of the city . For the first time in Edo recorded history, a foreign army occupied the ancient city of Benin.

As soon as the city was secured the main palace wall, hundreds of meters long and over four meters high, and several courthouses, mausoleums, and compounds adjacent to the wall, which the invaders called 'Juju' houses were all dynamited. All the sacred trees, which the invaders called 'Juju' trees, in the palace grounds that played very important roles in the city's cultural and socio-political routine were also dynamited. Among these were the Crucifixion, *Amufi*, *Esogban* and *Imaran* Trees. The Crucifixion Trees were two cotton seed trees, that were situated near a 20 metre-high tower, which had a 15-metre long bronze snake, *omwan se omwan*, a human is greater than another human, on its pyramidal roof. It was on this trees criminals were executed. The *Amufi* tree, also a cotton seed tree and was also situated close to the Tower. It was here the members of the *Amufi* guild, the guild of fish eagle hunters, performed aerial acrobatics that commemorates the legendary battle between an Edo legendary hero, Evian, and *Osogan*, a wing monster, during the *Isiokuo* (war readiness) festival. The *Esogban* Tree, which was also a cotton seed tree and was beside the official residence of the *Esogban*. The *Esogban*, is the *Iyase's* deputy, and also the kingdom's chief warlock and leader of all wizards and medicine men of Benin City. It was under the *Esogban* Tree that charlatan medicine man and magicians were executed. There were two

Imaran trees. One was also a cotton seed tree. They were planted during the reign of Omo N'Oba Eresoyen (r. c. 1735-1750) in front of the first *Imaran's* house. The *Imaran* is a non-hereditary war chieftain, and in old Benin before setting out for any campaign, every *Imaran* paraded his troops under these trees. These destructions were the first steps the British forces took in the deliberate and wanton destruction of the Benin Royal palace and royal quarters, the compounds of the city's high-ranking Ekhaemwen and many of the city's traditional landmarks.

The following day the looting and plundering began in earnest. It was an exercise that was carried out by all members of the Punitive Expedition, from the lowliest carrier to the highest-ranking officer. The marauders had expected a few 'ivory' in the palace, as envisaged by Phillips, but they found more than just ivory. The roofs of the palace's buildings were stripped of their copper and brass adornments, and the brass mnemonics plaques on the galleries pillars were ripped off. The massive brass snakes on the towers' roofs were also torn down, and the altars and shrines in the mausoleums were emptied of their brass and wooden memorial heads, ivory mnemonics and sacred artefacts of diverse material. The living quarters were also not spared. The wardrobes and treasure chests were emptied of their agates, coral beads, jewellery and ceremonial costumes. Even the harem's kitchens were stripped of their utensils. The building walls were demolished. The mud beds and tombs were dug up, and the treasures and valuables they contained were taken. This unprecedented pillaging is summed up in Dr Felix Roth words, '... a large part of the loot was found embedded in the walls of the houses'. The corrugated iron sheets removed from the living quarters of Omo N'Oba Ovonramwen were later used by the invaders to build their garrison on the grounds of the destroyed palace.

That afternoon a Royal Marine unit, accompanied by Rear-Admiral Harry Rawson went to *Uzebu* quarters, on the western outskirts of the end of the city. The unit looted and burnt down the palace of the Ezomo . The following day, the February 21, the palace of *Osodin*, a high-ranking *Okhaemwen*, on the eastern edge of the palace complex, was also looted and razed by a Royal Marine unit led by Commander Reginald H. Bacon. Then in the afternoon another Royal Marine and Naval units led by Captain Campbell went to *Uselu* quarters on the north-western outskirts of the city. There the unit looted the *Iyoba* (Queen Mother) palace, and then burnt it down. Thereafter, a group of sailors went to the already looted and vandalised Omo N'Oba's palace and set it on fire. In the words of an eyewitness, A. E. Lucy, a Royal Marine

Light Infantryman who was attached to the H.M.S. *Theseus*, in his logbook, '*The March to Benin and its Capture*', '... the next day (February 21) we went out to burn down the Queens Palace and our Bluejackets went out and burned down the King's Palace'. The centuries-old palace was reduced to a smouldering ruin, and the wall murals and motifs, and furniture and doors, which the looters could not take or overlooked, that depicted vital moments of Edo history or alluded to Edo origin, philosophy and mythology were lost forever.

The torching of the palace may have been a clumsy attempt to cover up the British Navy shameless looting of the palace or perhaps it was simply a manifestation of the destructive disposition of the civilising English men. To appreciate the scope of the invaders' depravity, the extent of the loot they stole and the scale of the unjustified damage they inflicted on Benin culture and civilisation, it is necessary to appreciate the size and significance of the palace to the Benin people. The palace complex, which then was about seven hundred years old, measured roughly two kilometres by one kilometre and was surrounded by an imposing corrugated wall about four metres high and one metre thick. It was literally a city within a city, the hub and nerve centre of the kingdom, and it comprised of hundreds of compounds, shrines, and galleries, whose pillars were adorned with brass and ivory plaques that chronicled the kingdom and city's history. The compounds, galleries and at least 34 sacred squares with *ugha* (mausoleum), were all linked together by a labyrinth of walled passages and formal gateways. The complex also housed all palace functionaries and retainers, including members of the various palace guilds and ceremonial sword bearers (*emuada*, sing. *omuada*), as well as household servants and slaves. There was also a very large harem, which was in itself a miniature version of the palace complex that was made up of ten streets and housed hundreds of queen consorts, (*iloi*, sing *oloi*), and their household servants and slaves. The palace was also the kingdom's central religious centre, and a grooming centre for many of the kingdom's vassal city-states' future kings

The principal individuals who instigated the events that led to the annihilation of Phillips clandestine invasion force were Major (later Sir) Claude Maxwell MacDonald, Major (later Sir) Ralph Moor, Captain (later Sir) Henry L. Gallwey and Mr James Pinnock. The others were, Edward Straw, the agent of Messers African Association Limited, Mr. Whitehead, the chief agent of Messrs African Association Limited, J.H. Swainson, the agent of Mr. James Pinnock, G.J. Greenshields, the agent of Messrs A. Miller Brothers and

Company, and Otto Bauer, the agent of Messer Bey and Zimmer.

The British and Niger Coast Protectorate officials who took part in the clandestine mission to abduct the king-Emperor of Benin kingdom, Omo N'Oba Ovonramwen, and pay for his abduction with the treasures expected to be found in his palace were Mr. James Robert Phillips, Major Peter Copland-Crawford, Captain Alan Maxwell Boisragon and Captain Arthur I. Maling. The others were Mr Ralph F. Locke, Dr Robert Elliott, and Mr Kenneth Campbell. The trading agents who took part in the unprecedented abduction and armed robbery venture were Mr Thomas Gordon of African Association Limited and Mr Harry S. Powis of Messrs Miller Brothers trading company.

The exact number of artworks, sacred artefacts, mnemonics and personal belongings of Omo N'Oba Ovonramwen, his mother, *Iyoba* Iheya, and Benin *Ekhaemwen* and citizens, which were stolen by the officers and men of the Benin Punitive Expedition, the exact quantity each thief stole and the whereabouts of most of the loot may never be known. However, it is a recorded fact that the under-mentioned individuals actively participated in the looting, plundering, and destruction of Benin City.

Allman, Robert. Dr Principal Medical Officer of the Benin Punitive Expedition.

Bacon, Reginald H. Commander (later Admiral) (Royal Navy)

Beaumont, G L. Captain (Royal Marine Light Infantry)

Burrows, Norman Captain (Niger Coast Protectorate Force)

Campbell. Captain (Royal Navy)

Carter, C.H.P. Captain (Niger Coast Protectorate Force)

Child. Captain (Royal Navy)

Copland-Crawford, Erskine

Cockburn. Lieutenant (Niger Coast Protectorate Force)

Daniels. Lieutenant (Niger Coast Protectorate Force)

Dibblee. Lieutenant (Royal Marine Light Infantry)

Egerton, G. Captain (later Admiral) (Royal Navy)

Erskine. Lieutenant. (Royal Navy)

Gabbett. Lieutenant. (Niger Coast Protectorate Force)

Gallwey, Henry L. Captain. (Later Sir) Vice-Consul Niger Coast Protectorate

Granville, Reginald Kerr. Lieutenant (Niger Coast Protectorate Force)

Hamilton, Bruce. Lieutenant Colonel (Niger Coast Protectorate Force)

Henniker. Captain (Niger Coast Protectorate Force)

Howe. Dr Medical Doctor.

Koe, Ringer. Captain (Niger Coast Protectorate Force)
Langdon. Major (Royal Marine Light Infantry)
Moor, Ralph D.R. Major (later Sir). Consul-General and Commissioner, Niger Coast Protectorate
Neville, George William. One of the founders of the Bank of British West Africa
O'Shee, R. E. Captain. (Royal Marine Light Infantry)
Rawson, Harry. Rear Admiral (Royal Navy) (Later Governor of New South Wales, 1902 - 1909)
Roche, T. Major (Royal Marine Light Infantry)
Robertson, Claude William. Captain (Royal Marine Light Infantry)
Roth Felix, Dr Medical Doctor
Roupell, E.S.P. Captain (Niger Coast Protectorate Force)
Searle. Major. (Niger Coast Protectorate Force)
Walker. Captain. (Royal Marine Light Infantry)
In March 1897, some part of the loot was sent as trophies to the Queen of England by Major Ralph Moor, Consul-General, and Commissioner, Niger Coast Protectorate. This is documented in the March 20, 1897, Niger Coast Protectorate official dispatch CSO 3/2/1, pp. 145-148 reports; Sir Ralph Moor to Foreign Office. Reporting the demands of Rear Admiral Rawson and his officers engaged in the Benin Expedition. Sends trophies to the Queen of England. CSO 3/4/1 Vol. 7, p. 82
Some of the museums and galleries that knowingly bought, collected and sold (and still sell) the stolen private belongings of Omo N'Oba Ovonramwen, Edo Ekhaemwen and citizens include:
Bankfield Museum, Halifax United Kingdom
British Museum London, United Kingdom
Catherine Reswick Collection Los Angeles
Glasgow Art Gallery and Museum, United Kingdom
Jesus College Cambridge
Leyden Museum United Kingdom
Liverpool Museum United Kingdom
Maidstone Museum and Art Gallery, Kent
Musee Barbier-Muller Genf Switzerland
Musee Picasso Paris France
Museum für Völkerkunde Berlin Germany
Museum für Völkerkunde Speyer Germany
Museum für Völkerkunde Dresden Germany

BENIN CITY: THE SACK THAT WAS

Museum für Völkerkunde Hamburg Germany
Museum für Völkerkunde Stuttgart Germany
Museum für Völkerkunde Munchen Germany
Museum für Völkerkunde Köln Germany
Museum für Völkerkunde Mannheim Germany
Museum für Völkerkunde Freiburg Germany
Museum für Völkerkunde Braunschweig Germany
Museum für Völkerkunde Vienna, Austria
Museum of Mankind, London United Kingdom
National Museum of African Art Pitt Rivers Museum, Oxford, United Kingdom
Science and Art Museum Philadelphia, USA
The Museum of Fine Arts, Houston, USA
The Metropolitan Museum of Art New York, USA

The number of Benin stolen artworks, mnemonics, religious and sacred artefacts, which were sold in the British Colony of Lagos as scrap metal is unknown, so also are those retained as souvenirs by officers and men of the Benin Punitive Expedition forces. The rest, 2400 pieces, according to British official figures, were taken to England and were later auctioned in Paris, France.

The breakdown of the sale in Paris is as follows: Austrian and German museums bought about 900 pieces. The museum in Berlin bought 580 pieces, Hamburg 196 pieces, Dresden 182 pieces, Leipzig 87 pieces, Stuttgart 80 pieces and Köln 73 pieces. The museums in Munich, Braunschweig, Mannheim, and Freiburg bought a total of about 95 pieces, and the museum in Vienna bought 167 pieces. St Petersburg museum in Russia: bought 40 pieces, the museum in Chicago in the USA, bought 33 pieces while British museums bought about 600 pieces. The London museum bought 280 pieces and Oxford Museum 327 pieces. The remaining loot were bought by private individuals.

COLONIAL OVERLORDS: THE VICTOR'S SONG

COLONIAL OVERLORDS: THE VICTOR'S SONG

'There was some doubt as to the white man sending someone beforehand saying he was coming.' -Dr Felix Roth. British Surgeon. 1897.
'... when a chief killed a chief, the chief must be killed.' -Major (later Sir) Ralph Moor, Consul General. Niger Coast Protectorate. 1897.

When Ebeikhinmwin, the heroic defender of Gwato, learned that Omo N'Oba Ovonramwen had abandoned Benin City, he marched up to the city only to find that his militia was no match for the well-entrenched and better-equipped Niger Coast Protectorate Force. So, Ebeikhinmwin unleashed his fury on the villages and settlements of *Ekhaemwen* who had surrendered and pledged their loyalty to the British occupiers. In response to the insurrection, the Niger Coast Protectorate Force commanded by Captain E.S.P. Roupell, the acting British Resident of Benin City: a brutal and murderous sadist, whom the Edo people nicknamed *amenhien* (pepper juice), embarked on a campaign of terror and bloodshed in the Gwato and Ugbine area, looting and destroying villages and settlements as far as Siluko and Okheluse some 50 kilometres Northwest of Benin City. Eventually, in May 1897, Ebeikhinmwin was captured and the uncoordinated resistance ended. The following month the resistance fighter was tried and sentenced to death. On June 24, 1897, the heroic defender of Gwato was hanged in front of the burnt out and destroyed royal palace.

Although Phillips' major objectives had been achieved: Benin City 'visited' (invaded and destroyed), the 'ivory' (Benin visual history, artworks, and sacred artefacts looted) in the king's house obtained. and a 'Native Council' set up in the 'obstruction's place, but the 'obstruction' (Omo N'Oba Ovonramwen) remained free. Efforts to capture him proved unsuccessful, and in all skirmishes with the Benin Royal forces, the Niger Coast Protectorate troopers were always forced to withdraw to the safety of their fort in Benin City. The Protectorate Authority, anxious to gain access to the hinterland, and members of the puppet Native Council, who feared reprisal from Benin resistance fighters, eventually resorted to diplomacy. Ultimately some members of the Native Council were able to assure Omo N'Oba Ovonramwen that the British would not harm him if he surrendered. So on August 5, 1897, the Omo N'Oba re-entered Benin City accompanied by some of his wives, loyal *Ekhaemwen* and the bulk of the Palace community.

COLONIAL OVERLORDS: THE VICTOR'S SONG

Two days later, on August 7, 1897, Captain Roupell summoned the Omo N'Oba to the Court House, which had been built on a part of the ruined palace's grounds, to formally surrender and make his submission. The British Resident strongly rejected entreaties by the Ero (one of the seven Uzama nobles) that the Omo N'Oba be allowed to make his submission in private. Captain Roupell was keen on humiliating the Omo N'Oba publicly to 'show the natives that the white men were the new masters of the land'. The vanquished Omo N'Oba had no choice, and so supported by two Ekhaemwen he made his formal submission to the Resident, who then officially deposed him as king of Benin. The Omo N'Oba's public humiliation prompted some high-ranking Ekhaemwen to commit suicide or migrate from Benin City.

Three weeks later, on September 1, 1897, the Omo N'Oba appeared before Major Ralph Moor's tribunal and accused of 'instigating' the killing of seven 'white chiefs'. Captain Roupell and Captain C. Carter, the Commanding Officer, Niger Coast Protectorate Force in Benin City assisted Major Ralph Moor, who was both prosecutor and judge of the tribunal. The trial was a paradox. It was a bizarre circus that was more pathetic than a kangaroo court. Three armed robbers were prosecuting their victim for defending his property against their break-in. Although Ralph Moor claimed that his inquest was in accordance with 'Native Laws and Customs' and thus only wanted to determine who instigated the 'killings' of January 4, 1897, the accused, Omo N'Oba Ovonramwen, had been presumed guilty and a cotton tree had already been earmarked for his execution. Furthermore, Ralph Moor's witnesses: Agamwonyi, Aigbedion, and Iguobaro, were themselves on trial.

Agamwonyi was a retainer of *Okhaemwen* Obaseki, while Aigbedion and Iguobaro were both retainers of *Okhaemwen* Obakhavbaye. Without doubt, the witnesses' statements were plea bargains because they were part of the Benin militia that annihilated Phillips' force at Ugbine. They testified that *Ologbose* Irabor, *Okhaemwen* Obaradesagbon, *Okhaemwen* Obakhavbaye, *Okhaemwen* Obayuwana, and *Okhaemwen* Uso were the only high-ranking Benin *Ekhaemwen* who actively participated in the destruction of Phillips' invasion force. Major Moor was no doubt very delighted with the 'testimonies' because it identified the alleged "Juju men" who were 'responsible' for the 'Benin Massacre'. He ordered the immediate arrest and detention of Obayuwana, Obakhavbaye, and Uso, including *Okakuo* Ugiagbe, the commander of the Ugbine border guards, who were present at the proceedings. Obaradesagbon had earlier committed suicide following the

Omo N'Oba's public humiliation, and *Ologbose* Irabor was leading the resistance war against the occupiers. That night, Obayuwana committed suicide in the cell because he could not bear the humiliation of detention, but Major Ralph Moor determined to 'show the natives the power of the white man', ordered Obayuwana's corpse to be hung in front of the ruined palace for a day. Some officers and soldiers of the Niger Coast Protectorate further desecrated the corpse by using it as a target practice.

Ralph Moor's tribunal revealed (a fact that Moor already knew) that Phillips had sent no message or messages to Omo N'Oba Ovonramwen of his intention to visit Benin City, and as Dr Felix Roth noted, 'There was some doubt as to the white man sending someone beforehand saying he was coming'.The hearing also showed the Omo N'Oba did not send any *Ekhaemwen* to Gwato to escort Phillips and his party into Benin City. Neither did he order any *Ekhaemwen* to kill Phillips and his party. Again as Roth asserted, a witness avowed, '... when the king was told the white men were coming, the king then called the people and told them the white man is bringing war... let them come and see me.... But the big chiefs overruled the king orders... and ordered the massacre of the white men'. Interestingly, Ralph Moor did not arrest *Iyase* Okizi, who was present during the proceedings, and whom, the defendants claimed ordered them to kill the intruding white men. In fact, the *Iyase* served as the chairman of Ralph Moor's Native Council from 1897 until his death in 1900.

In the end, quoting that according to the Native law, 'when a chief killed a chief, the chief must be killed', Major Moor ruled that seven native chiefs must die because seven white 'chiefs' had been killed. *Okakuo* Ugiagbe was 'pardoned' because he was 'young' or rather not a 'juju man', and *Ekhaemwen* Uso and Obakhavbaye were found guilty of 'actually' taking part in the 'killing' of the seven white 'chiefs'. They were condemned to death and hanged in front of the burnt out and destroyed palace. Thereafter Major Moor warned the other *Ekhaemwen* and nobles that if the *Ologbose*, the alleged 'chief instigator' of the 'Benin Massacre', was not handed over to him, he would personally hand-pick five *Ekhaemwen* and nobles, and execute them.

Meanwhile the principal accused, Omo N'Oba Ovonramwen, was neither pronounced guilty nor innocent. The truth was, Major Ralph Moor's policy dictated that vanquished 'native' rulers who were not hanged, were sent into exile. Concluding his bizarre circus, the Consul-General told the vanquished king was that he (the Omo N'Oba) and some of his loyal *Ekhaemwen* including their wives would be sent to Calabar or Lagos on a yearlong tour.

Then he ordered the Omo N'Oba not to leave the city but to report personally at the Courthouse with a response to the proposed yearlong tour on September 9, 1897. The proposal and restriction the Consul-General imposed on the Omo N'Oba's movement was a hint that Omo N'Oba Ewuare's prophecy was about to be fulfilled.

The Ezomo and some *Ekhaemwen* probably thought it wise to send the Omo N'Oba into hiding, but it was a poor error of judgement. On September 9, 1897, when Omo N'Oba Ovonramwen failed to turn up at the Courthouse at the appointed time and was not found by the armed unit sent to arrest him, Moor summoned all the high-ranking *Ekhaemwen* and nobles to the Courthouse. He threatened that if by the evening the Omo N'Oba was not handed over to him, he would burn their houses and kill all of them. The Ezomo had no reason to doubt Major Ralph Moor. He had witnessed the civilising white man's innate cruelty, contempt for the dead, and capacity to sow death and destruction on a large scale. The Ezomo quickly admitted that the Omo N'Oba was in his compound. Yet again, the Consul General had another opportunity to humiliate his defeated enemy. The Omo N'Oba was arrested, chained and detained like a common criminal. His wives were taken from him and handed back to their families, and finally, he was formally banished from Benin City for the rest of his life. This time the Omo N'Oba's humiliation was to impress on the Benin people the futility of resisting the white man's authority. All attempts the Omo N'Oba made to avoid the sentence, which included offering the Consul-General about 200 puncheons of oil palm produce and 500 ivory tusks (all which the Consul-General took) were rejected.

On the night of September 13, 1897, Omo N'Oba Ovonramwen was gagged, then strapped unto a hammock. He was taken out of Benin City escorted by a sixty-man unit of the Niger Coast Protectorate Force under the command of Captains Carter and Henniker. The deposed king was taken to Gele-Gele port and then transferred to a Niger Coast Protectorate yacht on the one-way journey to Calabar. On the way to Calabar, the Omo N'Oba was paraded about in shackles among the inhabitants of many settlements, villages, and towns to show them that the power of the 'Benin Juju has been broken forever'. In late 1897, Mr James Phillips' last objective was achieved when 2400 (official figures) 'ivory' 'found' in the house and City of the 'fetish king' of Benin were auctioned in Paris, France, 'to pay for the visit'.

In May 1899, after a two-year bitter resistance war, the Niger Coast Protectorate Force stormed the last bastion of the Benin resistance fighters at Okemue about 45 kilometres North-east of Benin City. In the ensuing encounter, five villages and an unknown number of settlements in the environs were completely razed. *Okhaemwen* Oviawe, one of the resistance commanders was killed, and the other two, *Ologbose* Irabor and *Okhaemwen* Ebohon were captured and put on trial. On June 24, 1899, *Ologbose* Irabor was pronounced guilty of 'instigating and actually taking part in the killings of seven white chiefs' and was summarily executed. *Okhaemwen* Ebohon was sentenced to a long prison term but was later pardoned.

The next year, 1900, the European four hundred-years old dream of political and economic domination of Benin kingdom was finally realised when a British company, Miller Brothers Company, established a trading factory in Benin City without the consent of a Benin king-emperor.

A FESTERING SORE: STILL I RISE

A FESTERING SORE: STILL I RISE

'A punitive expedition occupied the royal city of Benin in 1897. There in the Royal Palace, this expedition discovered the priceless treasures and took them back to Europe as spoils of war.' - Benin: Kings and Rituals. 2007.
'Kann man Amerika den Indianern zurückgeben?' - Director, Museum für Völkerkunde, Vienna, Austria. 2007.

Over the years, the details of the events that led to the invasion and destruction of Benin City have been deliberately distorted, falsified or suppressed. Apparently most writers, eminent scholars of African art history and history, and mainstream publications find it convenient to amplify the British government official version of the subject matter that 'Phillips as acting Consul-General had to pay a necessary visit to the Benin King in order to avoid resorting to the use of force and complete every peaceful means towards resolving the economic and political impasse in the Benin River region'. Hence it became widely assumed that January 4, 1987, Ugbine incident was an unprovoked attack on seven unarmed civilised British envoys and traders on a peaceful trade and diplomatic mission by primitive, savage and bloodthirsty Benin Chiefs. It also became an accepted fact that the Benin Punitive Expedition was a reprisal for the alleged January 4, 1897, killings of these alleged British envoys and traders. The amplification by writers, eminent scholars of African art history and history, and mainstream publications, without doubt, lent credence to the British government official position that the invasion, destruction, and looting of Benin City was an appropriate, legitimate and a justified venture.

In giving credence to the British government account that the alleged British envoys and traders were on a peaceful diplomatic humanitarian or trade mission and therefore were unarmed, it appears that these learned writers, professional art historians, historians and reputable mainstream publications have either not done enough research on the subject matter, or allowed prejudice to blind their senses of judgement and purposely omitted or falsified the accounts of the individuals or group of individuals who initiated or participated actively in the events that led to Phillips' mission of January 4 1897. This being so because their writings and publications make no references to Major Claude Maxwell MacDonald and Captain H Gallwey statements before and after the sham 'Treaty' of March 1892. Major

MacDonald, in the cover letter he sent with the original 'Treaty' to the Foreign Office, wrote, 'I hope before long to be able to put a stop to this state of affairs'. While Captain Gallwey remarked, 'I now consider that there will be no necessity to sent a punitive expedition to Benin City' Also they failed to mention Major MacDonald's statement after the apparent rejection of the treaty by the Benin king, which was '...The great stumbling block to any immediate advance being the fetish reign of terror which exist throughout the kingdom of Benin and will require severe measures in the future...' Also not mentioned or referred to are the aforementioned European traders' petitions, Phillips' November 17, 1896, letter to the Foreign Office, and the subsequent correspondences between the British Foreign Office, the Home Office and the Colony of Lagos.

Captain Alan Boisragon confirmed in his book, *The Benin Massacre*, that the idea to invade Benin City and topple the Benin king had been considered long before Mr James Phillips arrival in the Protectorate. He claimed that after the British Navy/Niger Coast Protectorate Force's invasion, looting and destruction of Broheimie Nana Olumo's trading settlement in September 1894, the Niger Coast Protectorate's Consul-General had considered invading Benin City in early 1895. Boisragon went on further to acknowledge that between September 1895 and early 1896 the Protectorate Force made at least two incursions into Benin territories. These aborted invasions are confirmed by the September 12, 1895, Niger Coast Protectorate official dispatch CSO 3/2/1, pp. 145-148 reports; Sir Ralph Moor to Foreign Office. Reporting on the abortive Expedition into Benin.

And again on February 5, 1896, Ralph Moor forwarded a supplementary list of men who took part in another Expedition on the Benin River to the Foreign Office. These aborted invasions were also acknowledged in the book *Great Benin: Its Customs Art and Horrors*, where it is stated, 'Several British officers made attempts at various times to get into Benin territory but they were invariably met by armed forces'. Indeed one instance of these hostile intrusions was mentioned in the book, *Nigeria Under British Rule*, where the writer claimed, 'In August of 1895 Consul-General Moor directed one of his officials Mr Copland-Crawford to endeavour to open up relations therewith and to visit the king and town'

Boisragon also acknowledged that the failed Phillips' mission was not an unarmed diplomatic mission. He claimed that the British military officers' revolvers were locked in boxes carried by 'African porters', and maintained that when Benin militia surrounded Phillips' purportedly unarmed, peaceful and humanitarian party, the British officers would have been able to put up some effective resistance had Phillips not given the order: *No revolvers, gentlemen!* Dr Felix Roth, in his diary, as well confirmed that the Phillips' mission was an armed expedition. He contended that some of the weapons the Benin militias used against the Benin Punitive Expedition forces were undoubtedly the repeater rifles they had captured from the Phillips' clandestine expedition. In his diary entry of February 18, 1897, Dr Roth wrote, '... by the ping of the bullets the natives (Benin defenders) must be using repeating rifles, the firing so heavy and quickly delivered'. Again in his diary entry of February 19, 1897, he contended that no arms and ammunition were found among the remains of Phillips' mission belongings, which were recovered in a gallery in the Benin king's palace. He thus concluded, '... the natives had most probably used them against us'.

Another account claimed that when the advance-guard of the Benin Punitive Expedition's Main Column was confronted by Benin irregulars at *Unueru* quarter in the southeastern part of the city, on February 19, 1897, the invaders were said to be screaming: 'They (the Benin irregulars) are using repeaters! They are using repeaters!' Moreover as one account of the alleged 'Benin Massacre' claimed, 'The porters were being massacred in the rear, and the Europeans ran back to get their revolvers out of their boxes'. One other account contended '.. the expedition left for Benin ... with their firearms locked securely in a chest'. And according to R.S. Billett, '...The officers of the Niger Coast Protectorate Force that accompanied the expedition were advised they could take their revolvers....'. Indeed the *International Herald Tribune* expressed some doubts about the news that the Phillips mission was unarmed. And according to the publication, 'The fact that the officers composing the mission to Benin having proceeded totally unarmed is inexplicable, especially as the chief of Benin City was known to be hostile to the British.'

Nonetheless, our learned writers, eminent scholars of African art history and history, and reputable mainstream publications continue to endorse and propagate the British government created myth and disinformation that the Phillips failed abduction and robbery venture was a peaceful, unarmed diplomatic and humanitarian mission, and the destruction of his clandestine invasion force was a massacre. In addition, these eminent scholars of African art history and history, and mainstream publications continue to propagate the spurious claim that Benin City was accidentally razed by a fire and that the city was not looted by men and officers of the Benin Punitive Expedition

Forces when the city was captured or 'seized' as some of these scholars would say. In the article, *Benin: The Sack that never was*, for instance, the writer contends that the Benin king's palace and the city were not plundered. In his view, the Benin king's palace was accidentally burnt down by a fire set off by some African porters. According to the respected art historian, '... the fire that burnt down the Oba's Palace was started by the Expedition's local porters who were playing with gun powder about three-quarters of a mile away from the gates of the Palace'. In the book, *Benin: Kings and Rituals*, it is claimed, 'a fire broke out which destroyed the palace and most of the city.' And the writer further asserts that 'A punitive expedition occupied the royal city of Benin in 1897. There in the Royal Palace, this expedition discovered the priceless treasures and took them back to Europe as spoils of war'. In the words of an art historian, in his book, *African Art*, 'the British Royal Navy seized a vast quantity of bronze casting and ivory carvings as reparation in the course of the Punitive Expedition'. While in the book, *Royal Art of Benin: The Perls Collection*, the writer contends, 'the Benin Punitive Expedition captured Benin City, destroying much of the palace and town in the process. The thousands of the artworks found in the palace were seized'. The author of the book, *Black Africa: Masks Sculpture and Jewellery*, argues that the British invaders did not destroy the Benin king's palace. In her opinion, the palace had been burnt down earlier back in the 17th century. R.H. Bacon in his book, *Benin: The City of Blood* claimed that Benin artworks, mnemonics, and sacred artefacts were not looted but were found 'abandoned lying in the dust of ages'. While in the book, *The Art of Benin*, the contention is, 'Many of the plaques now in the British Museum were collected during the British Punitive Expedition in 1897'.

The eyewitness accounts of some individuals, who participated actively in the capture, looting, and destruction of Benin City between the February 19 and 21 1897, however, tell a different story. And the accounts include the writings of Dr Felix Roth, Commander (later Admiral) R. H. Bacon and Trooper A. E. Lucy, and the visual records of Dr Allman and Lieutenant R. K. Granville (photographs), Captain (later Admiral) Egerton (paintings) and Mr Seppings, a journalist (sketches). Dr Felix Roth's accounts first appeared in, *The Halifax Naturalist*, June 1898, and then in, *The Reliquary*, July 1898. And later it appeared (reprinted from the *Journal of the Manchester Geographical Society*) in the appendix of his brother's *Great Benin: Its Customs Art and Horrors* (1903). Commander (later Admiral) R. H. Bacon's account is documented in his book, *Benin: The City of Blood*, which was published in 1897, while that of A.E. Lucy's account is in his logbook, *The March to Benin and its Capture*, which was published in 1900.

Commander R. H. Bacon, an eyewitness and active participant in the destruction of Benin City records, 'On February 20 a strong party accompanied by the Admiral, (Rear Admiral Rawson) went to burn Ojomo's (Ezomo) compound. He further states, 'Early next morning (February 21) I was sent with a strong party of Houssas (Hausa) and the Theseus sailors and marines to burn Ochudi's (Osodin) compound'. And his records for that day ended with the report: 'The same afternoon a large party under Captain Campbell proceeded to the Queen Mother (*Iyoba*) House and destroyed it...'. Dr Felix Roth and Trooper Lucy were more candid in their accounts. Corroborating Bacon's account about the deliberate, mindless and wanton destruction of Benin City, Lucy wrote, '... the next day (February 21) we went out to burn down the Queens,(*Iyoba*) Palace And then added (what Bacon refused or 'forgot' to mention)... and our Bluejackets went out and burned down the King's Palace'.

In acknowledging the massive plundering of Benin City by the British Navy and Niger Coast Protectorate Force, Roth stated, '... a large part of the loot was found embedded in the walls of the houses'. Again it seems these learned and respected eminent writers, art historians, and historians, including mainstream publications are unaware of these information or overlooked them.

Interestingly, several photographs by Dr Allman and Lieutenant R.K. Granville that were taken immediately after Benin City was captured, which are on display in the British Museum, appear in the publications of some of these writers, art historians and historians. And these include *Art of Benin, Treasures of Ancient Nigeria, Royal Art of Benin: The Perls Collection, Great Benin: Its Customs Art and Horrors, The Art of Benin, Benin: Kings and Rituals* and *An Introduction to Benin Art and Technology* just to mention a few. And also according to two curators, Jeremy Coote and Elizabeth Edwards in an article, *Images of Benin at the Pitt Rivers Museum: African Arts, Autumn 1997* many eminent scholars and experts of African art history and history have long had access to the Egerton's paintings since they were first exhibited at Maidstone Museum and Art Gallery, Kent, between 1975-1984, and also at the Pitt Rivers Museum since 1991. Captain Egerton's paintings were done right inside the Benin palace, where he and his Commander in Chief, Admiral H Rawson, bivouacked between February 19 and 21 1897.

In spite of the wealth of information, these eminent scholars and experts of

A FESTERING SORE: STILL I RISE

African art history and history, and mainstream publications continue to claim that the January 4, 1897, defeat of the Phillips' clandestine invasion force was a massacre of unarmed British envoys and traders, which they labelled 'Benin Massacre'. They continue to insist that the brazen plundering of Benin artwork and treasures was a 'collection', 'confiscation', 'discovery' or 'seizure', and maintain that the deliberate destruction of the Benin king's palace and most of the city by the British forces was an accident.

Whatever these eminent writers, scholars, experts of African art history and history, and mainstream publications choose to write or comment about this chapter of Benin history, the truth is that they know Phillips' mission was neither a political nor a trade venture. They know the mission was not about persuading the Benin king to allow Europeans unrestricted access to Benin City. And they know the mission was not a humanitarian venture aimed at stopping the 'trafficking and massacring of slaves'. These eminent writers, scholars, experts of African art history and history, and mainstream publications also know that Phillips sent no messages beforehand to the Benin king of his intention to visit Benin City. They know his mission was an unauthorised and murderous abduction and armed robbery undertaking that was against all rules of hospitality and conventions of international relationship. They know beyond doubt as R.S. Billett candidly pointed out, 'This mission (Phillips') was not a religious crusade, it was an attempt to get the King to open up the Edo tribal lands to British traders, and submit to British rule,.....King Overami (Ovonramwen) refusal to allow trade was seen as an affront to the authority of the colonial administration and Phillips advised the Foreign Office of his intention to visit the King of Benin, and deal with him'.

The eminent writers, scholars, experts of African art history and history, and mainstream publications know the Benin king's palace was not burnt down in the 17th century or destroyed accidentally in the process of the city's capture. They know that the razing of the Benin king's palace, that of his mother and those of many high-ranking Ekhaemwen were deliberate, dastardly and barbaric deeds carried out by officers and men of the British Royal Navy and Niger Coast Protectorate Force. The eminent writers, scholars, experts of African art history and history, and mainstream publications know that the Benin sacred artefacts, mnemonics, and works of art were looted and not 'discovered', 'collected', 'found accidentally' or 'seized to discourage the practice of human sacrifices by the Benin people'.

A FESTERING SORE: STILL I RISE

The eminent writers, scholars, experts of African art history and history, and mainstream publications know that the high-ranking officers of the punitive expedition did not buy Benin treasures in any auction but participated actively, just as well as the expedition's rank and file, in the shameless plundering of Benin City. Dr Roth wrote, 'a curious brass jug... I obtained out of the wall at the back of the king's compound'. Also, a procurer of Benin artworks claimed that a bronze leopard pendant, which he purchased in 1955 for a museum, was 'brought to Europe by one of the expedition's high officers'. There are publications that reveal virtually all the expedition high-ranking officers brought their loot from Benin City to England and in addition, there are photographs showing some of these officers displaying their stolen treasures of Benin on their return to England. Furthermore, in the *Twenty-sixth Annual Report of the Jesus College Cambridge*, in July 1930, it was acknowledged that George William Neville, who took part in the Benin Punitive expedition, presented to the College a 'splendid bronze cock of ancient native workmanship', which he brought back to England. Many personal belongings of Omo N'Oba Ovonramwen including ivory chests, ceremonial coral beads and attire and hip masks (one of which was chosen as the symbol for the 2nd Black Festival of Art and Culture in 1977) were stolen by Major Ralph Moor, Admiral Rawson, Captain Egerton and Captain Henry Gallwey. It is a documented fact that Captain Egerton brought to England at least thirty-three Benin works of art, sacred artefacts and mnemonics. While Dr Allman stole many ancestral staves including a number of bronze dwarfs (two of which are now in the Museum für Völkerkunde, Vienna Austria). Major Erskine Copeland-Crawford and Lieutenant R.K. Granville to mention a few are said to have each brought to England a substantial number Benin works of art, sacred artefacts and mnemonics. Captain Norman Burrows on his return to England was photographed proudly showing off his stolen Benin treasures, which were labelled curios. Besides the denial, distortion or omission of Phillips' real motives, the conflicting versions of the Ugbine incident and denial of the deliberate looting and destruction of Benin City, some of these eminent scholars and experts of African art history and history also came up with what they claim were 'factors' that contributed to the Ugbine incident. And these include 'the timing of the Benin ague rituals', 'massacring of slaves', 'Phillips' obstinacy', 'Benin kingdom's dwindling economic and political fortunes', and the 'military threats of the Nupe kingdom and the city-state of Ibadan'. However when the European traders' petitions, the Niger Coast Protectorate dispatches, Phillips' request, and the Foreign and Colonial Offices responses are all considered, the prejudices and hypocrises of these writers, art historians and historians become apparent.

The assertion by one expert of African art history that 'all members of the Phillips mission except Boisragon and Bacon were killed against all rules of hospitality and conventions of international relationship' is quite interesting. The impression conveyed by the writer is quite obvious. Her insinuation that the Edo people are primitive savages who had no regards for hospitality, human lives, and human relationship is nothing new. She is simply echoing the racist and conceited sentiments of her predecessors: 19th and 20th-century experts of African art history and history.

If it is assumed that Phillips sent messages to the Benin king of his intended unarmed, peaceful and diplomatic visit, as our learned art historians and historians have portrayed, the questions are: What was the Benin king's reply to these messages? Was the Benin king prepared to receive a Niger Coast Protectorate official at that particular time? According to several publications, the Benin king was making a 'big Custom and could not receive any Protectorate official'. Indeed even Phillips himself, in his November 17, 1896, letter, asking for permission to visit Benin City and depose the Benin king, wrote, 'The Jakri Chiefs ... asked the King to receive a Government officer. His reply was that he was making a big Custom to last four months and could not do so until it was over'.

It should not be forgotten that as far back as June 1896, Phillips' immediate boss, Major Ralph Moor, had promised Mr James Pinnock that 'an expedition would be sent in January or February 1897 to remove the king and his juju men from the country'. And also as mentioned in the book, *Nigeria Under British Rule*, after Copland-Crawford's aborted mission, 'Moor advised that in the dry season another peaceable attempt should be made to open up the country, and if this was not successful, then, if need be force should be used'. So why then did this courageous and high-minded civilised gentleman decide to embark on his 'visit' in early January 1897, which he himself has planned for February 1897? And why was he not deterred by the warnings of friendly *Itsekiri* Chiefs not to embark on his peaceful mission? As earlier pointed out, 'A local *Itsekiri* Chief, Dogho, advised Phillips it would be suicide to proceed', and '... Chief Dudu warned the Benin king was making "country custom" and he would not allow any white man to enter the city'. Is it within bounds of all decency, hospitality and international relationship for an individual (forewarned, uninvited, unwanted and armed with hostile intentions) to forcefully impose a visit on an unwilling host? So who broke all rules of hospitality and international relationship? A forewarned, uninvited, unwanted and armed hostile British marauders, with blood in their hands, and abduction, murder and robbery in their hearts or Benin chiefs with all moral obligations to protect their kingdom territorial integrity?

The claim by another expert of African art history that 'the timing of Benin *ague* rituals' catalysed the events which, led to the 'Benin Massacre' is quite amusing. As earlier pointed out, in June 1896, seven months before the Benin ague rituals for the Edo year began, Major Ralph Moor had promised Mr. James Pinnock that in January or February 1897 (the time the Benin *ague* rituals are held) an expedition would be sent in to remove the (Benin) king and his juju men from the country. Then again in November 1896 acting, Consul-General Phillips informed his superiors in Whitehall of his intention (which was approved by his boss Major Moor who on holidays was in England) to visit Benin City in February 1897 and depose the king of Benin. He was aware of the fact that the Benin king was making "big Custom" that would last until February 1897 as confirmed in his above-mentioned letter. It is also a documented fact that in January 1897 Phillips was well warned by two *Itsekiri* chiefs that the Benin King was making "country Custom". How then could have the timing of the Benin ague rituals, a ceremony, which is celebrated annually in January, catalyse the preplanned events? Is this professional art historian insinuating that the Benin king should have postponed the *ague* ceremony, so as to allow a white man to come to Benin City, kidnap him and then steal his property to pay for the kidnapping?

In March 1896 the European traders who were operating in the Benin River area themselves claimed that their livelihoods and those of their *Itsekiri* partners were wholly dependent on the trade (oil palm) that comes from the king's country. They also went on further to say, '… there is a future before the Benin River'. Yet an expert of African art history and history claim that Benin kingdom's 'dwindling economic fortunes' played a major role in the events that led to the Ugbine incident. If the kingdom's economic fortunes were dwindling why would the Benin king refuse to trade with the *Itsekiri* middlemen? And why would the European traders make so many desperate and incessant appeals to the Niger Coast Protectorate authorities to 'open up' Benin territories for trade? Beyond any doubt, the Benin kingdom's economy was not dependent on trade with the Itsekiri middlemen or their European financiers. On the other hand, it was the Itsekiri middlemen and their European financiers who were dependent on the kingdom's natural resources and whose economic fortunes were dwindling. As a matter of fact, Benin kingdom was practically a self-sufficient kingdom, and in the words of a 19th century European trader, 'Benin does not need Liverpool', the then economic and industrial power hub of England.

Another expert of African art history and history also claim that 'massacring of slaves', what some other experts call 'the infamous aspect of Benin history', catalysed the events that led to the invasion and destruction of Benin City. Did the 'massacring of slaves' catalyse the invasion and destruction of Brohiemie, Nana Olomo's settlement? Unfortunately, the expert chose to forget that the 'massacring of slaves' as he says was practised at one time or the other by all cultures, including his. Even then, if it is assumed, as the expert insinuated that the practice was exclusive to the Edo people, was it then also an infamous aspect of Benin history to put unarmed slaves against wild beasts or heavily armed gladiators in public arenas? Was putting padlocks in the mouths of slaves working in sugar plantations also an infamous aspect of Benin history? Was it an infamous aspect of Benin history to show compassion to enemies by giving them smallpox infected blankets to sleep on? Was it also an infamous aspect of Benin history to make tobacco pouches from the breasts and genitalia of vanquished enemies? Was it an infamous aspect of Benin history to attack 'primitive' kingdoms, burn down their towns and villages, loot their treasures and then hang the rulers for resisting 'civilisation' or conversion to Christianity? Or was burning alive men and women who were accused of witchcraft also an infamous aspect of Benin history?

How would these western writers, scholars of African art history and history, and mainstream publications react to German publications, which claimed six million that Jews died in the 'process of their being taken to concentration camps'? How would these western experts of African history and art history, writers and mainstream publications respond when a German writer claims that German armies occupied the cities of Europe, and there in the cities these armies discovered Jewish priceless treasures and took them back to Germany as spoils of war? How would they react to Serbian reports that eight thousand Muslim Bosnian men and boys died in Srebrenica during 'process of the town's capture' by Bosnian Serbs troops? How would they respond to a European art historian's claim that the 'timing of a Jewish festival and Heinrich Himmler's obstinacy' catalysed Nazi SA storm troopers infamous Crystal Night or Night of Broken Glass, of 9th -10th November 1938? Which German historian would claim that the artworks and personal belongings of Jews, which the Nazis apparently looted during the Second World War, were legitimately acquired? Which European art collector would donate his collections of stolen Jewish sacred artefacts, artworks and personal belongings to a European museum? Which European or American museum, gallery or auction house will openly exhibit, buy or sell the stolen artworks, religious and sacred artefacts of a European nation or the personal belongings of a European monarch? Which European or American museum will rebuff a European nation's monarch request for the return of his or her nation's stolen artworks and religious artefacts, and then sell the articles at rock-bottom prices to private collectors? And which European art historian or writer will proudly claim that Reinhard Heydrich was killed by Partisans Czech and Slovak against all rules of hospitality and conventions of international relationship?

The British official mindset, which was expressed in the book *Great Benin: Its Customs Art and Horrors*, that Benin City deserved her fate, the "little war" (the Benin Punitive Expedition) was justified and the treasures of Benin was legally acquired because they were 'obtained by the shedding of British blood' has not changed over the years. The attitudes of the buyers, resellers, and receivers (directors and curators of museums, galleries and proprietors auction houses) of the Edo people stolen treasures have also not changed. In the 1950's when the Nigerian Government made a request for the return of some of the stolen Benin treasures that are in the British Museum, a director of the museum stated 'History cannot be unravelled', and then he added, '...visitors expect to see these things on display in the British Museum.' In the late 1990's Omo N'Oba N'Edo, Uku Akpolokpolo, Erediauwa, the great-grandson of Omo N'Oba N'Edo, Uku Akpolokpolo, Ovonramwen made a similar request to the Glasgow Art Gallery and Museum Scotland, the United Kingdom for the return of the stolen Benin treasures that are on display in the museum. Again the request was turned down, and the museum director's reply was: 'We are not in the business of redressing historical wrongs'. Once more in 2007, replying to a similar request by the Benin monarch, the director of the Museum für Volkerkunde Vienna, Austria answered, *'Kann man Amerika den Indianern zurückgeben?'* (Can America be given back to the Native Americans?)

The mindset of the scholars and experts of African art history and history about the events that led to the January 4, 1897, incident at Ugbine have also not changed. Comments such as 'all members of the Phillips mission except Boisragon and Bacon were killed against all rules of hospitality and conventions of international relationship', 'the Benin Punitive Expedition captured Benin City, destroying much of the palace and town in the process', and 'a punitive expedition occupied the royal city of Benin in 1897. There in the Royal Palace, this expedition discovered the priceless treasures and took them back to Europe as spoils of war', simply demonstrate a shameless and vicious disinformation campaign that endorses the British government official position. A position that is committed to the suppression of the actual roles played by the Niger Coast Protectorate officials of what actually led to alleged 'Benin Massacre'. These storytellers need to be told plainly that the distortion of events that led to this incidence at Ugbine, and the denial of the deliberate and wanton destruction of Benin City is tantamount to the denial of the Holocaust, the Wounded Knee and Sharpeville massacres. It is important to refresh their memories that the denial of the Holocaust in most European countries, is considered a serious crime, and carry severe consequences. And in these countries, individuals who deny the Holocaust are deemed to be impenitent and inconsiderate liars. It is not out of place to say individuals who knowingly distort or fabricate provocative and spurious stories about the January 4 Ugbine incident, the invasion, looting and destruction of Benin City are in any way different.

The directors of museums and galleries, and proprietors of auction houses that procured and sold (and continue to sell) Edo peoples' stolen treasures, and proudly pronounce: 'history cannot be unravelled', 'we are not in the business of redressing historical wrongs' or 'Can America be given back to the Indians?' need to be reminded that the looting of artworks during times of war has been outlawed since the Napoleonic Wars, and the restitution of looted works within Europe have been enforced ever since. And also they should not forget that the buying, possession, and sale of stolen goods are criminal offences according to universally accepted international laws and those of their individual countries. It is essential to call the attention of these directors, and proprietors of auction houses, to John Henry Merryman's article, *Imperialism, Art and Restitution*. In the article, Merryman wrote 'the seizure of works of art by the Nazis in the occupied countries was classified as war crimes at the Nuremberg International Military Tribunal because the victorious Allied powers (France, Great Britain and the United States of America) claimed that the confiscation of private property by aggressive occupying powers violated international laws.' According to Merryman, Alfred Rosenberg, the man who was in charge of German art-looting operation, was charged at Nuremberg with 'the looting and destruction of works of art'. Rosenberg was found guilty of this crime and was hanged.

Interestingly the British officials who instigated the events that led to the 'Benin Massacre', including those who took very active part in the premeditated plundering and destruction of Benin City were (and still) honoured as civilised, courageous and high-minded gentlemen. The Edo people whose civilisation was deliberately destroyed were (and still) portrayed as murderous primitive bloodthirsty savages without regards to hospitality and rules of human relationship by these 'eminent scholars' of African art history and history, and western mainstream publications. The Edo peoples' capital city, Benin City, they named, 'The City of Blood' or 'City of Skulls'. And the Edo king-emperor whose palace was burnt down, personal belongings stolen, and subjected to all indignities and then exiled from his land by those who brought death and destruction was christened 'grinning Black King' by a reputable western mainstream publication. The writers who fictionalised the Ugbine incident and as well as those who continue distort the facts about the episode are referred to as 'eminent scholars' of African art history and history, and the directors of museums that are knowingly and unlawfully keeping (and are not prepared to return them to the rightful owners) the looted sacred artefacts, treasures and visual history of the Edo people are called 'Custodians of mankind treasures' by western publications One does not expect American and European experts of African art history and history, mainstream media and publications to be objective and write differently on the subject matter as their 19th and early 20th century predecessors did. Hence comments such as the looted treasures of the Edo people were 'collected', 'discovered', 'found', 'seized' or 'taken', are not unexpected. As the Edo says, *Egui setin ze ihinron ne ovbiere ze ikpakpa*, The Tortoise cannot have a shell, and one expects its offspring to have a skin. Incidentally Trooper Lucy's in his aforementioned Logbook, stated, 'In the wake of these actions arrived Mr Seppins (Seppings Wright of the Illustrated London News). So it just shows how reporters get hold of things that happen if he had been there and seen for himself perhaps the London papers would not have been so full of lies'. And sadly the these lies just continue to be told well into the 21st century. Until these writers, art historians and historians, and mainstream media and publications that retold (and continue to retell) British government created Ugbine incident myth dare write this sad chapter of human history as it really happened, in the perception of the Edo people they remain perceived as liars and pseudo-historians.

A FESTERING SORE: STILL I RISE

It is also essential to mention that while many governments, galleries, and museums all over the world, are returning the looted properties of many other ethnic peoples, the British government, and the museums and galleries that are holding on to the Edo peoples stolen treasures have adamantly refused to do so. The British government attitude is not unexpected since she lacks the moral courage to face up to the evils of her colonial past in Benin kingdom, and the damage her disinformation campaign has inflicted on the Edo people psyche. Also not unexpected are the attitudes of the museum directors who arrogantly say; 'history cannot be unravelled', 'we are not in the business of redressing historical wrongs' or 'Can America be given back to the Indians?' And these attitudes can only be summed up in the Edo saying: *A gha we egbe oyi, a ghi we egbe imarie*, A barefaced thief, is a barefaced liar. Until all the stolen sacred artefacts, artworks and visual history of the Edo people are returned to the rightful owners, the British government, the directors and curators of American and European museums and galleries, and proprietors of Auction houses, including the descendants of the actual looters that hold on to (and sell) these treasures, in the perception of the Edo people, will remain perceived as thieves and receivers of stolen goods.

POSTSCRIPT

You may write me down in history with your bitter twisted lies
you may trod me in the very dirt but still like dust I will rise
- **Maya Angelou**

POSTSCRIPT

CREDITS

CREDITS

Aisien, Ekhaguosa
1996. Benin and her Neighbours. Benin City

Aisien, Ekhaguosa
2006. The Edo man of the 20th Century. Benin City

Becky, Ceravolo
2005. The Looting of Nigerian Art and Antiquity. The theft of Patrimony in Nineteenth Century Benin. Introduction to African Art.

Ben-Amos, Paula
1980. The Art of Benin. London.

Billett, R.S.
2001. "Captain C W Robertson (RMLI)". Military Historical Society of Australia.

Boisragon, A
1898. The Benin Massacre. London.

Cathy Midwinter
1994. Benin: an African Kingdom. World Wide Fund for Nature.

Coote Jeremy and Elizabeth Edwards
1997. "Images of Benin at the Pitt Rivers Museum" African Arts autumn (no 4) pages 26-35.

Crowder, Michael
1978. The Story of Nigeria. London.

Curnow, Kathy
1997. "The Art of Fasting: Benin's Ague Ceremony" African Arts autumn (no 4) pages 46-53.

CREDITS

Egharevba, Jacob
1968. A short history of Benin. Ibadan, Nigeria.

Esse, U.O.A.
1988. Catalogue of the Correspondence and Papers of the Niger Coast Protectorate. Enugu, Nigeria.

Eweka, Iro
1998: Dawn To Dusk: Folk Tales from Benin. New York.

Ezra, Kate
1992. Royal Art of Benin: The Perls Collections. New York.

Geary, William N. M.
1965. Nigeria Under British Rule.

Geo Epoche
2014. Issue 66 . Article: Die Magie der Kriegerkönige: Afrika. 1415- 1960.

Gott, Richard
1997. Article 'The Looting of Benin' The Independent Saturday 22 February 1997.

Lucy, A. E
1900. A logbook 'The March to Benin and its Capture'.

Merryman, John Henry
2006. Imperialism, Art and Restitution. New York.

Meyer, Laure
1992. Black Africa: Masks Sculpture and Jewellery. Italy.

Okpoku Kwame
2007, Article Opening of the exhibition "Benin kings and Rituals, Court Art from Nigeria" Vienna, Austria.

CREDITS

Oronsaye, Aiyevbekpen Katherine
Personal communications.

Oronsaye, Leonard
Personal communications.

Plankensteiner, Barbara
2007. Benin kings and Rituals, Court Art from Nigeria

Roth, Henry Ling
1968. Great Benin: Its customs Art and Horrors. (1903) Reprint New York.

The Guardian
2017. August 12, Article: Museums In Talks To Return Benin Bronzes To Africa.

The International Herald Tribune
1997. January 11, Article: 100, 75 and 50 years ago.

The New York Times
1897. January 22 ,Article: The Massacre Near Benin.

Time Magazine
1935. December 16 Arts: City of Blood.

Time Magazine
1965. August 6 Arts: The Bronzes of Benin.

Tong, Raymond
1993. The village of ghosts Contemporary Review. Vol. 263.

Website: www.richardlander.org.uk
Article: Benin Bronzes.

CREDITS

Willet, Frank
1973. African Art.

Willet, Frank and Eyo Ekpo
1980. Treasures of ancient Nigeria. New York.